Angels Without Wings

Angels Without Wings

A Courageous Family's Triumph over Tragedy

Jane Vonnegut Yarmolinsky

Thorndike Press • Thorndike, Maine

Library of Congress Cataloging in Publication Data:

Yarmolinsky, Jane Vonnegut.
  Angels without wings.

  1. Yarmolinsky, Jane Vonnegut. 2. Yarmolinsky, Jane
Vonnegut – Family. 3. Disasters – Psychological aspects.
4. Family – Mental health – Massachusetts. 5. Massachu-
setts – Biography. 6. Large type books. I. Title.
[CT275.Y26A3 1988]   974.4'043'0922 [B]   88-2235
ISBN 0-89621-140-1 (alk. paper)

Some of the material in this book previously appeared in
Family Circle.

Large Print edition available in North America by arrangement
with Houghton Mifflin Company.

Cover design by Norma Whitman.

TO MY TWO HUSBANDS

Without Carl
these things would not have
been part of my life.

Without Adam
I could not have written
about them.

Contents

PART THREE

Publisher's Note

When Jane Vonnegut Yarmolinsky wrote this book, she was forcing herself to confront one of the most difficult periods of her life, a time when her ability to accept what life demanded of her was put to a severe test. In order to deal with her painful but remarkable memories, she began writing in the third person, calling herself Eve and changing some, though not all, of the names of the other people in the story. Occasionally, she unconsciously slipped into the first person, using "I" and "me" when she was speaking of Eve. Three quarters of the way through the story, she changed entirely to the first person, explaining the transition this way:

> I cannot hide behind "Eve" any longer. Eve was necessary until now, partly because I really did almost have to turn into someone else in order to become the mother of four more children so suddenly. And in writing [the story], I

needed someone else to talk to. But now Eve has served her purpose. I will miss her. I could not have done it without her. But now I am ready to admit that I am really Jane. Me. Jane.

I have no idea how this will turn out.

It is clear from this that Jane's use of the third person was a device, one often used by writers to distance themselves sufficiently from their difficult experiences so that they can begin getting them down on paper. But the first-person narration seemed more appropriate to the intimacy of the story, and it was our judgment that, had she lived, Jane would have wanted that voice throughout the book, for the sake of consistency and accessibility. Thus, we have converted the balance of the book to the first person, which makes the entire story as intimate as the last quarter. (We have also changed the names of all the rest of the people in the book, to protect their privacy.)

What emerges, then, is a voice full of awe, self-doubt, wisdom, warmth, and love, an irresistible voice that speaks *from* the heart and *to* the heart. Houghton Mifflin* is proud to be

---

Angels Without Wings was first published by Houghton Mifflin Company in 1987.

giving readers the opportunity to hear her voice.

★

We would like to express our gratitude to Rod MacLeish for his contribution to this book. Despite many commitments of his own, Mr. MacLeish took on the task of responding to our editing of *Angels Without Wings* in the author's stead, making many constructive suggestions.

A new commandment I give to you, that you love one another; even as I have loved you, that you also love one another. By this all men will know that you are my disciples, if you have love for one another.

JOHN 13:34-35

What potions have I drunk of Siren tears,
Distill'd from limbecks foul as hell within,
Applying fears to hopes, and hopes to fears,
Still losing when I saw myself to win?
What wretched errors hath my heart
  committed,
Whilst it hath thought itself so blessed
  never?
How have mine eyes out of their spheres
  been fitted,
In the distraction of this madding fever?
O benefit of ill! now I find true
That better is by evil still made better;
And ruin'd love, when it is built anew,
Grows fairer than at first, more strong,
  far greater.
  So I return rebuk'd to my content,
  And gain by ills thrice more than I
    have spent.

WILLIAM SHAKESPEARE, Sonnet 119

Part One

Part One

1

September 15, 1958

Our stability is but balance, and wisdom lies in masterful administration of the unforeseen.
Robert Bridges
The Testament of Beauty

It was Monday morning, and even the old house seemed to know the summer was over. It takes until two weeks past Labor Day for summer to truly end on Cape Cod, before the last weekend guests pack their bags and go away, before the fun lovers stop swarming in the west end of Hyannis, and before you have become accustomed to the school bus collecting the children from under the horse chestnut tree on the corner at 8:05. The old house seemed to sigh along with me as it disgorged the children through the rarely used front door, just barely in time. Was it a sigh for the spent summer? Or for lost youth? Or was it just a breeze coming through the house from a different direction? Or what? My oldest child, Matt, mounting the school bus steps, looked back quizzically, as if he wondered, too.

I couldn't have said.

Carl and I and our friends the Roths from Connecticut had had a pleasure-filled weekend: good food, long talks, drinking late; a last swim in the already icy water of Sandy Neck; a brisk walk down the trackless beach at least halfway to the abandoned lighthouse, where, tucked away next to a clump of beach grass, we had found a pile of discarded paperbacks and movie magazines. We sportively lugged them home, congratulating ourselves on our good fortune, as if they were a treasure we had been looking for. When we got home, all salty, sandy, windblown, and invigorated, there was time and enough hot water for showers all around, then the last hamburgers of the season grilled outside, and Irish coffee between games of Ping-Pong on the big, sagging front porch. We watched with satisfaction the heavy Sunday traffic steadily streaming by on Old King's Highway, on its way off the Cape. And finally, the Roths, the last guests of summer, packed their belongings and children into their station wagon and joined the stream of cars going back to the real world. The Roths were good friends, but Carl and I were glad to see them go. We had had enough fun. We had a real world to deal with, too.

So, when that Monday morning came, and Nelly, age four, had been dropped off at nursery school, and twelve-year-old Matt and eight-year-old Amy had gone off too (already adjusted to the confinement of school in that miraculous way children have of adjusting), it was definitely time for the grown-ups to make a similar accommodation. Time to face a new season, whatever it might hold, and start a new project. Time to clean up summer's residue: sandy beach towels and stiff sneakers, snarled fishing line and seaweed, seashells, crumbled sand dollars, and horseshoe crabs. *Do all that and* then *sit down at the desk,* I was telling myself as I started the tedious annual process. *Get it together. Collect your wits. Pay the bills.*

When the grandfather clock (bought by Carl's father on a trip to Germany in 1923) in the corner of the suddenly empty living room struck ten o'clock, that's what I was doing: sitting at my desk, paying the bills that had accumulated over the summer like the seaweed. The radio was playing softly in Carl's study off the living room, the music occasionally interrupted by an indistinctly heard news report. The familiar clackety-clack of his typewriter was steady

17

enough that I knew he, too, was getting down to work.

I could tell by the rhythm of the typewriter that the work was going well. It was about time. Ever since the previous February, when he had finally gotten an advance on the book he had been working on for two years before that, Carl had been struggling to finish it. March, April, and May had been fairly productive months, our spirits buoyed by the advance and by the sale of a short story earlier in the winter. But the distractions of the summer had brought work almost to a halt. Weekend after weekend, vacationing friends and relatives and friends of relatives would show up — a well-known hazard of living on the Cape — and many of them wouldn't go home on Sunday night, not seeming to understand that the house was also a place where a man had to make a living, for God's sake. The kids' noisy comings and goings added to the tumult. Carl had to handle all of this in the face of a deadline. It was an old story. We had lived with it for years. It's what we talked about at cocktail parties on the Cape in the summer.

The time had gone pleasantly enough, actually. Which, of course, was the problem. Pleasure at that house was always getting in the way of the serious business of life. It was a sparkling mix of fun and high anxiety laced with neurosis. When you added the stress of reality — like not having enough money to pay the bills — who could stand it?

Carl and I could, that was who.

We had proved that by sticking with it year after year. We were agreed that writing was a most disagreeable way to make a living, that Carl might have to give it up and go into teaching or real estate or public relations or something, anything. This was before the days when a young family might reasonably have pursued the alternative of the wife going to work. Who would take care of the children? There was no money for babysitters. There were no community child-care centers, no family nearby. I had no immediately marketable skills, and the word "househusband" had not been coined yet. Without really questioning them, we instinctively clung to the traditional roles — husband the breadwinner, wife the homemaker — though in each case there was unacknowledged rage at the limitations. It was a question of survival. Carl had tried other occupations when our income dwindled to practically nothing. He sold cars, took P.R. jobs, did brief stints with publications of one sort or another, and taught at a school for disturbed children. But none of these forays into the outside, workaday world turned out very well, and he always ended up back at the typewriter, in agony.

That's what he was good at. "It's all I can do," he would say to interviewers, sometimes sheepishly, sometimes proudly, sometimes in anger, always looking somewhat mystified. His was an utterly original, unique talent. No one else wrote the way he did, though some tried years later. I thought it an important talent, prophetic and true, bordering on genius. I was proud that I had perceived this before anyone else did. I had fallen in love with him largely because of it. I knew it was only a matter of time before he would get the recognition he deserved and the material rewards that would come with it. That was my stance: Belief, with a capital B, in him and in our future. It kept me going. Some of it even rubbed off on him, although he never would have admitted it. Cheerfulness in the face of adversity was not his mode. He preferred a kind of ironic desperation, blended with fits of manic mirth. Which was what kept *him* going. That and the agony. And lately he had discovered the flotative quality of alcohol.

In whatever proportion, the mixture of confidence, cheerfulness, desperation, hilarity, irony, and alcohol had worked pretty well. Our marriage had survived all kinds of severe rattlings and bad bends, had produced three beautiful, bright, healthy, and reasonably well-behaved children, and no one had actually gone hungry yet. What more could or should anyone expect, all things considered? Well, a lot.

The checking account was very low, I noticed, snapping out of my congenital reverie. I had spent at least two weeks not noticing. So I would pay what bills I could. If I could only get the paperwork out of the way, maybe there would at last be time to get started on some more creative project. I had long dreamed of the time when I could have a few hours a day to myself, to do a little writing of my own; that is, if I could remember how to put a sentence together, and if we could afford a second typewriter.

No chance, I thought, looking at the swiftly dwindling balance in the checkbook. As soon as I paid the mortgage, the excess water bill, the electric bill, and the life insurance premium, there wouldn't be enough left over for food, much less a new typewriter. Unless something sold. There were always stories out making the rounds. I had papered a wastebasket with rejection slips a few years earlier, but things were better now. At any rate, the sounds from the study were reassuring.

I was continually on the alert for whatever

little clues I could pick up. As I tuned back in to the clatter of the typewriter, I could feel my tension slipping away. I drew a long breath of relief. Normalcy at last! *Keep on trying,* I murmured to myself. That was our motto. No matter how difficult it got trying to turn words into commodities, the thing was to keep on trying. That's what the three white candles in the three miniature wine bottles on the kitchen mantel were about: one for *keep,* one for *on,* one for *trying.* So be it, I thought. If he can do it, I can do it. At last we will have some peace to do it in.

The door between the living room and the study suddenly flew open, its loose hinge complaining as Carl loosened it still more. Shoulders hunched, he strode purposefully through the living room on his way to the kitchen. I was puzzled. When his work was going well, he usually waited until later to take a break. He was already halfway through the dining room when I asked, "What're you doing?"

"Calling Ned."

Ned Willis was Carl's brother-in-law. He lived in New Jersey and was a trade publications editor in New York City. Usually we waited until the evening to call, when we could talk to both Annie, Carl's older sister, and Ned at home, and when the phone rates were down. I heard him dialing, eleven digits for the long distance call to Ned's office. Maybe Carl had an idea for Ned's new project, a magazine for the adhesives industry. The thought made sense to me. This might be part of the intimations of new beginnings that I was feeling. I returned to my juggling act with the checkbook. The grandfather clock struck the quarter hour.

Moments later, Carl went back through the living room. There had been only brief murmurings from him on the telephone.

"Get him?"

I knew he couldn't have, or he'd still be talking.

"Too early. He's not in yet."

Carl went back into the study, closing the squeaky door behind him.

Even though Annie had not been feeling well lately, she and Ned might have had a farewell-to-summer celebration over the weekend too, so Ned might have been late getting off to work.

The typewriter began again immediately, as if there had been no pause at all, no interruption of thought. I was right. He was into something good. He hadn't even stopped to make a cup of coffee. Good for him. A wave of affection swept over me as I realized how much in tune our moods were.

Our new year had always started in the fall, not in dread January, ever since we had gotten married on September first. We had celebrated our anniversary only two weeks earlier. We had made it through thirteen years! The fourteenth was bound to be better. Happy new year, Sweetie, I beamed through the study door, wondering whether in our magical symmetry of mood he would catch it. The typing didn't stop. I wondered which of the three current projects he was working on: the book, the new short story, or the rewrite of the TV script. I hoped it was the book. That was the only one he really liked, but working on it was a luxury when we were so short on cash.

As I turned the page for 1958 in the big black ledger, a stray thought tickled the back of my mind. Carl had never, as far as I knew, called Ned at his office. There must be some good reason. He would tell me at noon.

At a little after twelve, the groaning door announced Carl's re-emergence from the study. I realized that I was starving. We went out to the kitchen together, both satisfied with a good half-day's work. We found a can of tomato-vegetable alphabet soup. There was something vaguely comforting about all those letters float-ing around, waiting to be put into words.

Just as we sat down to the soup, looking

forward to finding out how each other's morning went, the telephone rang. Carl answered it. I started my soup. Carl said things like "Yes, this is he," and "Yes, that's all right." The preliminaries finished, he fell silent. I looked up at him, trying to gauge the expected length of the conversation. His expression told me nothing. Then he gave a long, low whistle. I kept staring at him, but he would not meet my eyes. Then, with his back to me, he finished the conversation.

"Yes, I will. Of course. You too. I'll call if I hear anything."

He hung up and turned around, but still he wouldn't look at me. The color had drained out of his face. He leaned against the counter, making no move toward his chair. The silence continued. Finally, I couldn't stand it anymore.

"Say something."

When he looked at me, his face was still blank.

"A commuter train went off an open drawbridge in New Jersey this morning," he said.

We stared at each other, trying to deny what we could not know but did: Ned was on that train and he was dead.

We had no reason to be as certain as we were. The call had been from Ned's office in New York. His partner was worried because Ned hadn't shown up that morning. He'd called

Carl, wondering if Ned and Carl had a plan to meet somewhere that day, since Carl had called earlier in the morning. He hesitated to mention the freak drawbridge accident on the Jersey Central that morning. Ned never took that train. But he wasn't home, and he wasn't at the hospital visiting Annie. They couldn't find him anywhere. He always called in if he wasn't planning to come to the office. Ned's partner had asked Carl why he'd called that morning.

But, sitting in the kitchen, looking at his cold soup, Carl couldn't figure out why he'd called Ned's office. He only knew that, as the Jersey Central accident was happening, he *had* called Ned. Now he knew that Ned was dead.

We didn't find out until later, listening to the radio, exactly when the train went off the drawbridge. Ned's partner hadn't mentioned the precise time, thinking it didn't matter. But I knew it did matter, that the train had gone into Newark Bay between 10:10 and 10:15. For reasons I could not explain, I had been watching the clock that morning and was vividly aware that that was when Carl had placed his call. It was no surprise to hear on the news that the accident had occurred at precisely 10:13.

Lunch forgotten, we walked out to the mailbox to pick up the morning mail.

"If what we think is true is true, it's the

god damnedest most unfair thing I've ever heard of," Carl muttered. Angry animation had returned to his face.

Deep down, I harbored a conviction that there must be some *reason* for what had happened, incapable as we might be of comprehending what that reason could be. The facts were not all in yet. The truth was only partially known. But, on the face of it, I had to agree with Carl.

Ned's partner had also mentioned that Annie was in the hospital, assuming that we knew that. We had known she wasn't feeling well, but not that she had been hospitalized. Carl called the house in Rumson to find out about it.

A babysitter taking care of twenty-one-month-old Paul answered the telephone. She reported that Annie had gone to Monmouth Memorial Hospital "for tests" on Sunday night. Ned had left for the city a little later than usual that morning because he had to pick up the babysitter and get some groceries first. He planned to visit Annie at the hospital later that day, on his way home. The three older boys were off at school, as usual. They were all fine. John had a little runny nose, but nothing serious. She expected them home around three-thirty. She gave us Annie's phone number at the hospital, but Carl didn't call Annie. He got on a plane for New York instead.

As we waited on the nearly deserted airstrip in Hyannis for Carl to board the two o'clock flight to La Guardia, I said quietly, "If it's as bad as we think it is, bring them back."

That was all that was said. But it was decided.

I stayed close to the radio for the rest of the day, listening to the reports of the train accident that filled the airwaves. It was the most newsworthy thing that happened on the eastern seaboard that day.

Divers were searching Newark Bay for bodies. No names of victims or survivors had been released yet, pending notification of next of kin.

Matt and Amy came home from school, Nelly from her best friend's house down the street, and immediately they all went back out into the bright September afternoon to play. I decided to tell them nothing, though it was hard to disguise my distraction. At twelve, eight, and four, they were too young to be told the bad news, at least before anyone could be sure exactly what it was. They barely knew their cousins, and were only vaguely aware that they had an uncle named Ned. It made sense to them that their father had gone to New York on a business trip. He often did that. I went numbly about cleaning up the kitchen, starting their supper — the saving grace of routine.

My mind rambled helplessly, then focused on my nephews, also home from school by now. To what? What could they know by now? What could they be thinking? Who would take care of them? I started to cry.

I wandered around the house, found myself staring out the living room window at a large, oblong marble slab we had found in a junkyard once, which was leaning against the unused part of the house, the old summer kitchen. When he couldn't write words on paper, Carl went around carving them on things — wood, cement, brick, plaster, marble. He literally wrote on the walls. Several years ago, with an old chisel and hammer, he had carved into the marble slab the final words of *Ulysses:* "...and his heart was going like mad and yes I said yes I will Yes."

"Yes I will, yes I will, yes," I said to the cold marble slab. It was a seduction, an acceptance of an altogether different sort from what Joyce had in mind.

When Nelly came flying into the darkening living room and wanted to know why I was crying, I couldn't tell her.

"I guess I wish Daddy didn't have to go to New York, darling. But he'll be back soon."

I realized that my deepest fear was that he

might never come back. I had never been afraid of accidents before, but now I was. I was exhausted by the range of the day's emotions. Would our early morning new beginning be for nothing? How could we be so sure that Ned had been killed? What had made Carl pick up the telephone at that precise moment? What was the matter with Annie? What was going on? What was I supposed to do about it?

No answers came. Not then, anyway.

2

July 15, 1958

"It's a poor sort of memory that only works backwards," the Queen remarked.
Lewis Carroll
Through the Looking-Glass

That night, lying awake, I remembered a strange dream from the past summer. All dreams are strange, of course, but this particularly oppressive and terrible recurring dream had come to permeate even my waking hours and eventually to characterize the very condition of my being for a period of weeks.

The dream first appeared around the fifteenth of June. From then on, time and again, it recurred at exactly three o'clock in the morning. The image in my mind's eye was of a huge red sun. It became clear that there was incredible life and energy in the enormous, fiery, red-golden sphere that filled my entire conscious-

31

ness. The sphere was exploding, ever expanding, yet ever the same. It seemed as though the explosion would have to reach a crescendo and then taper down, but it never did. The globe just kept expanding. Again and again, I woke up at precisely three in the morning, terrified. What kind of apocalyptic vision was this? It was so consistent, it must mean something. Had I dreamed the end of the world? In those days, as in these, it did seem as though the world might be coming to an end.

I knew nothing of dream interpretation then. Awake, my brain kept trying to rationalize this looming image. Was it a cancer cell? Yes, it was an enormously magnified human cell, cancerously exploding. There had to be a connection between this cell and the sun, because in the dream they looked so much alike. Cancer is exploding suns, limitless energy. Or the sun, which is exploding energy, is a cancer. But no, the sun is life-*giving*, not -taking. Depends on how close you are to it, doesn't it? I looked up *Cancer* in the *Columbia Encyclopedia*. In Latin, the crab. In astronomy, the constellation lying on the ecliptic — the sun's apparent path through the heavens — between Gemini and Leo. Long ago, the Tropic of Cancer was named for the constellation, because the sun was in Cancer at the time of the summer solstice. I looked up *summer solstice:* about June 22. *Solstice:* sun stands still.

But why this dream that was more like a psychedelic hallucination? Why me? Why then? Why with such intensity, in the middle of the night, every night, disturbing my sleep and my waking hours as well? What was I supposed to *do* with this horrifying, somehow secret information, deviously imparted to me by my unconscious in the dark of the night? My practical side had the idea I was supposed to *do* something with everything.

I hated it, this awful, sick, exploding ball of fire. It was too frightening even to tell Carl about. Which was what turned it into a secret. He might think I was crazy. So I kept my exploding sun to myself, as I often kept things I was afraid of to myself. I became more and more reluctant to go to sleep for fear of the dream. I became an insomniac.

Although Carl and I had been told earlier in the year that his sister had cancer, I made no conscious connection between that suppressed, never-referred-to knowledge and my dream. Gradually, as the summer progressed, I devised a strategy for dealing with the nightmare. I programmed myself to wake up as soon as it started happening. But by then I was so shaken that I couldn't get back to sleep. I would get out of bed the instant my eyes opened, very quietly so as not to awaken Carl, who was invariably deep in his own noisy dreams, rumbling like a freight train. I would swallow a tranquilizer, put on my bathrobe, go out to the kitchen, make some chocolate milk, drink it, and read something innocuous for a while. After about an hour and a half of this, in the preternatural silence of the slumbering house, I was usually so sleepy that I had to go back to bed. The exploding sun never returned after I started this routine. But I feared it would if I didn't watch out. It got so that I would wake a little before three in anticipation of the explosion, thereby short-circuiting it. Thus I learned to outwit this specter of the night, and thus my insomnia grew.

Once the sun no longer invaded my dreams, I found I could talk about it to Carl. But I knew how boring other people's dreams could be, unless you were an analyst and they were paying you to listen, so when he wasn't particularly interested, I wasn't particularly surprised. He had other things on his mind and rightly so. I stopped trying to explain.

Then, that same summer, other strange things started to happen. I woke up one morning wanting to know where the refugees were.

Carl didn't know how to deal with this. He

began to look at me rather oddly, I thought. I realized I'd have to find out for myself.

I went out to the barn one hot July day looking for the refugees, but there was no sign of them. It was filled with garbage cans, heaps of old newspapers and magazines, broken-down furniture, and a variety of aborted artistic projects. Chunks of ancient matted straw still clung to the rough-hewn beams, testimony to its long-ago days as a working barn. I never crossed the threshold without thinking: someday I'm going to fix this place up, someday I'm going to live here.

But that day it was more important to find the refugees. I went back to the house, across the uneven backyard where the weeds were winning, and up to the attic. This was a much better place for the refugees to hide. There was a lot of clutter up there, but it was a more comfortable kind of clutter. There were a lot of homey things about the attic, with its peaked ceiling, its old hand-pegged beams, the hiding places under the eaves, and the nice bricked area where the chimney went up straight through the middle. It was before I put clothes bars up for out-of-season things, so there was much more space then than now. It was really possible to imagine cozy little rooms up there, a special living area for the refugees.

In fact, there were some frayed and torn old blankets in a heap in one corner. I made a neat pile of them, thinking, someday when I have more time, I'll bring a needle and thread up here and mend them.

I went back downstairs and tried to put my mind to the life of the household — plans for the summer day, the comings and goings of my husband and children, making a picnic lunch, answering the telephone, sorting the laundry — being a good wife and mother. But all I could think about was the refugees, about getting everything ready for them. They hadn't come yet, but I knew they were on their way.

I decided it would be best not to mention the refugees again to Carl, and certainly not to the children. The fact that I wasn't at all sure who the refugees were, or where they were, had nothing to do with my decision not to talk about them. I just knew my family would not understand. They were all too young to understand, including Carl.

When I went back up to the attic for something, forgetting the minute I got there what it was, I found that the most tattered of the blankets I had piled neatly, the white one with the baby blue satin binding, was mended! I picked it up in wonder, remembering distinctly a long, jagged tear right down the middle. The tear was not there anymore. I accepted this phenomenon instantly. A simple little miracle had occurred in my attic. I must prepare myself for others.

That night after dinner, while Carl and the kids were playing games in the living room, I slipped upstairs and put a glass of milk, some crackers, a jar of peanut butter, and a knife on a plate at the top of the attic stairs.

I was excited when I went to bed later, having figured out how to cope with the problem of the refugees. The sun did not come up in my dreams that night. In the morning, the milk and the crackers were gone. I didn't tell a soul. I knew the refugees were not ready to come out yet.

Then I began to notice the words on the floors. In a house with children there are many word games: letters and words on cardboard, on blocks of wood, on colorful pieces of paper. Children come home from school with their art work in clumsily stapled-together pockets of bright construction paper, saying HAPPY HALLOWEEN MOM AND DAD. Things like that. And then the passage of time slowly disintegrates the paper, and the letters and words left behind float around the house, especially upstairs, mingling with other letters and words and pages torn out of books, rearranging themselves into new words, new messages, new pages — out of whose book? It was as if these words and letters had a life of their own. It was as if the whole upstairs had a life of its own, *and it was trying to tell me something.*

The house was alive! I wandered from room to room while the children were outside, trying to clean up but really struggling to understand the messages. I was very careful not to disturb anything for fear of destroying a message before it was complete. As I watched, cautiously spacing my visits upstairs so as not to embarrass the refugees by inadvertently coming upon them before they were ready, the messages began to take shape.

But they were in Russian, of all crazy things. I got out my old Russian grammar book from the course I'd taken at George Washington University in 1945. But it was no use. It seemed these messages were full of mistakes.

The situation was beginning to be really upsetting. It occurred to me that if I told Carl the whole puzzling story, he might be helpful. Probably there was some obvious explanation that I was just stupidly missing. Clearly, someone was trying to tell me something *important,* something that merited being *understood,* and I was being so dumb. But I was afraid to tell Carl. I couldn't have said what I was afraid of.

I began to read the papers more carefully for news of what was going on in the Soviet Union. This thing, whatever it was, belonged to a larger world.

On the fifteenth of July, after days of keeping all these fantastic speculations to myself, I woke up early in the morning absolutely certain of the answer. The refugees out in the barn had had a baby. I had put the milk in the wrong place, and babies don't eat peanut butter. How *stupid* of me! Someone had mended the blanket in the attic for me to take out to the baby in the barn, and then had *told* me in Russian what to do. But I had been so dense. I hadn't caught on.

I didn't wait to get dressed. I got up, went to the attic, got the blanket, and took it out to the barn. But the baby wasn't there. The barn was the same as ever; all that mess and no sign of a baby.

Suddenly I felt sick. I had made some terrible mistake. I could hardly drag myself back to the house and into bed, my legs and arms were so heavy. I lay in bed, numb, stiff, and scared to death. One simple thought ran through my head again and again: I had failed. I had truly failed. If I had one more thought with this faulty brain, I might ruin everything. If I hadn't already. I moaned aloud.

Carl turned over in his sleep, woke up, and

wanted to know what the matter was. I found it excruciatingly difficult to make my lips form words. But I managed to whisper to him that I was afraid, so afraid. The baby wasn't in the barn. Where could the baby be?

Carl got up and called the doctor.

Well, damn, I thought, I knew the jig would be up if I told. But how could I not tell, now that it had become so important? Where on earth could the baby be?

I felt a sharp stab of pain in my lower abdomen. My God, he's not born yet. So that was it! A surge of relief swept over me. At last I understood. The baby was coming, and I had been told to get ready for him. All right. The barn would be ready, and the attic too, if that seemed to be the right place when the time came. We could put a space heater up there. By the time he was born, which would be Christmas Eve, it would be too cold in the barn, anyway.

But it had been all right in a barn the First Time. Why not this time? Well, times have changed. All that had become purely symbolic by now, I thought. "They" had given me the symbols to help me comprehend what was going on the second time around, this Second Coming. I certainly could not have understood without reference to the symbolism of it all. Because, for one thing, I could not possibly be pregnant – not at thirty-six after three children, not when I had been so careful since Nelly was born almost four years ago.

As I lay there immobile, my mind racing, battling with the incomprehensibility of my predicament, the doctor arrived. It was a little after eleven-thirty, after his morning rounds at the hospital in Hyannis but before lunch. I could still relate to another reality, but I could not speak. There was simply no way to describe what was going on in my head. If I was even to try, they would surely cart me off to the nearest loony bin. Carl hovered anxiously at the bedroom door, having told Dr. Simmons what little he knew. Dr. Simmons sat next to the bed for a few minutes, looking at me after he had taken my pulse and temperature. He didn't try very hard to get me to talk.

"Poor Jane," he said finally. "Something out of your past has frightened you." He talked to Carl in the next room and found out that I had not been sleeping or eating very well. He gave me a shot of something – I never found out what – and said it would make me feel better. He ordered me to go to sleep and left.

But how could I sleep when there was so much to do? I was forgetting that it wasn't December yet. I had to get out to the barn. It was imperative that this birth come to pass in the

41

right place, otherwise how were people going to understand it? Clearly, I was not capable of telling them; even if I were, no one would believe me. The symbolism was everything.

I drifted off to sleep, my Bible, which I always referred to in times of crisis, beside me. It was open to Luke 2:12: "And this will be a sign for you: you will find a baby wrapped in cloths, and lying in a manger." I dreamed, wondering whether it would be a boy or a girl. Maybe a girl this time?

When I awakened from my drugged sleep some five or six hours later, everything was different. The shot had worked like a miracle mind conditioner, which, like miracle hair conditioner, got all the tangles out. My sense of urgency had dissipated. I knew I didn't really have to get out to the barn. There was no baby there, and there wasn't going to be. My abdomen was flat. There were no pains in it. But I was exhausted.

Later that evening, while Carl was feeding the kids, thinking I was still asleep, I went up to the attic just to look around. The mended blanket was there in its corner, but it lacked the marvelous soft glow it seemed to have when I perceived it as a miracle. It was just an old worn blanket in an attic corner. I had probably mended it one day and then forgot. On the way back downstairs, I looked for words on the floors. The children's books and games and toys were scattered around randomly, as they had been for years. I could connect an *N* in one room with an *O* in another, if I worked at it, for *NO*. But the Russian was gone. I couldn't find a single *NYET*.

Nuts, I thought. At the same time I was relieved to have been somehow returned to the world of substance that I was used to. It had been kind of fun — while it lasted — to peer over the brink at my own madness. But it was time I came back.

Occasionally, as the summer waned, I would wonder what *that* had been all about. But real life picked up and went on, and gradually, as the real days and weeks went by, I was absorbed in the manifold activities of a busy family and a steady stream of visitors, and forgot those disoriented, unreal midsummer nights and days.

Until September 17.

3

September 17, 1958

Everyone can consider the open ways of God's Providence, but there is this other way, full of meanders and labyrinths, the more particular and obscure method of his Providence, a serpentine and crooked line whereby He draws those actions His wisdom intends.
Sir Thomas Browne
Religio Medici

Wednesday morning around ten, well after the children had left for school, the phone rang.

I knew it would be Carl. I had been waiting for his call all day Tuesday, all night, and all that morning, dreading it, knowing he would call when he could, unable to think about anything or do anything. Immobilized.

"Annie died last night."

I could hardly breathe for the hearing of it,

44

the words that described what I already knew. It was as though those words had been filling the air all along. Annie had died at midnight. Her last words were "No pain." She died almost exactly thirty-six hours after her husband.

It took a long time for me to piece together what had happened in New Jersey during the past thirty-six hours, what those hours had been like for Carl, for the boys — and what they must have been like for Annie. It all had to be sifted through so many grief-numbed memories, over such a long period of time. As it turned out, the shock of it numbed the boys' memories permanently. Years went by before they could tell me the bits and pieces they did remember.

Even the adults' memories of what happened when, who was where, and who said what to whom are monumentally confused. Carl thinks Sara, Ned's older sister who lived in Summit, New Jersey, met his plane and drove him to Rumson. Sara doesn't remember that; she says she went straight to the house. Carl thinks his brother, Arnold, who arrived at some point from Weston, Massachusetts, went with him to the hospital that first day, but Arnold couldn't have, because he was still on the road from New Mexico on Monday and couldn't have gotten to New Jersey until Tuesday. Carl says no one was home but the babysitter when he got there; the boys say they were all there. Sara says she got there first. Carl says a Catholic neighbor was taking care of the kids; Sara says it was Winnie, the black woman who had been babysitting all day. Carl thinks Annie died the same day Ned did; John, the second oldest of the four boys, thinks it was three days later.

Clearly, all the available brains were hopelessly scrambled. Minds do strange things to time in situations like that (and maybe at all times). No computer recorded what happened. So the computer that is the human imagination will have to do. My imagination, after listening carefully for twenty-seven years, put it together this way:

John was the first one home that Monday. His sixth-grade civics class customarily listened to the eleven o'clock news on the radio and then commented on it. The news that day was all about the terrible train accident. It hadn't occurred to John that his father might have been on that train — since Ned always took the early train — until that afternoon on the school bus when he sat next to a little girl who was crying because she was sure her father had been on it. John did his best to comfort her and persuade her she was mistaken to think that. When he got home, the babysitter told him not to worry, but there had been a call from his father's office saying his father hadn't come in that morning. Suddenly the girl's fears did not seem so silly. He went upstairs to his bedroom window, which had a view of Sailor's Way as far as the curve, and willed with all his eleven-year-old strength for his father's old beige car with the wooden sides to come around the curve.

The news had spread through Cubby's school as well, and he arrived home with a feeling of creeping doubt, deepened now by the news at home and John's anxiety. Cubby was nine.

By the time Ned Jr. got there from high school, having no idea that anything was wrong, both his little brothers were in tears. His response was anger. He told them to stop being ridiculous crybabies. There was nothing to cry about. Anger and denial came first, then fear. But he couldn't cry. He was the oldest, and someone had to be in charge. He called his father's office to find out whether there was anything to this wild rumor and found out that there was. Then the terror set in. He called me in Barnstable and found out Carl was on his way. He called Aunt Sara in Summit, an hour away, and learned that she was just leaving and would be there as soon as possible. He was still furious with his brothers for being such babies, which was his habitual reaction to tears. But if there was nothing to worry about, why were the aunts and uncles rushing to Rumson?

Ned and John walked to the end of the lane, to where Sailor's Way met the main road. They often went there to meet their father at the end of the day. They sat silently on the split rail fence by the side of the road, looking to the left, to the curve in Rumson Road where you could first tell a car's color. Their hearts rose several times as beige cars rounded the curve, but it was never the right one. Finally they turned and walked back down the now sunless, empty lane; no scuffling behind the old station wagon, tagging its fenders, racing it to the driveway. Ned, no longer angry, thoroughly sobered, tried to calm John's fears by saying that their dad was probably staying late in New York because of his big new deal with the adhesives magazine. But they both knew that if that were true, their father would have called by then. So they just dropped the idea instead of talking about it to Cubby, who was outside whistling at the birds. Cubby went quietly back to doing his homework. He had a math test the next day and wanted his dad to be proud of him. It was almost dinner time, but who would cook?

Carl arrived at the house earlier than Ned Sr.

would have if Ned had come home that night. He had a hard time explaining himself, since the official word was that no one knew anything. Then the baby started crying so hard that no one could concentrate on what anyone said anyway. It was a chaos of repressed emotions and unspoken fear. Neighbors started arriving with food. Carl made sure the babysitter would stay and then left for the hospital.

Annie was glad to see him. Carl wondered how she could be glad about anything. She looked terrible, in a way she had never looked before. She hadn't wanted her brother to see her like that. She always seemed beautiful before, to him and to everyone else. Now she was bent over like a question mark.

"Where's Ned?" was the first thing she said to him.

Carl had to say he didn't know.

And that's how Annie found out.

She had seen an extra edition of the paper that morning, with headlines about the train wreck, before a nurse took it away from her. No one could explain to her why her husband had not come to see her. No one tried. As the hours passed, and still he hadn't come, and still he didn't call, the cold certainty grew and grew in her, submerging the other cold certainty that was growing in her, that the cancer was killing her. "Not yet, please God," she must have thought, "not yet." But still he didn't come, and still he didn't call.

So when Carl appeared in the door of her hospital room instead of Ned, Carl who was supposed to be on Cape Cod, Annie knew that Ned must be dead. No one had to tell her. If her husband was alive, he would be there and her brother would not be. It was that simple.

She couldn't say so, of course. She asked for a cigarette, which she was not allowed to have. The doctor said she could have one.

After a while they made some brother and sister jokes, jokes they had been tossing back and forth at each other all their lives. There was a whole string of them:

"I keep thinking this is Monday."

"Well, it is."

"That's what I keep thinking."

"Do you know Mike?"

"No, what's his name?"

"Who?"

"Mike."

"I never heard of him."

"What did you say?"

"I didn't say anything."

"Oh, I didn't hear you."

Annie asked what would happen to the boys if both she and Ned were to die. Carl answered that the boys would be well loved and well cared for and well educated, and that they would be kept together.

It was a promise.

It was so simple, at that point.

Later that evening when Carl was back at the house in Rumson, friends began to gather. Neighbors materialized out of the dark. The phone kept ringing: neighbors, friends, and relatives from far away wanting to know whether Ned was all right, afraid to ask but needing to know. Everyone was relieved to find that Carl (and Sara by then) was there, but at the same time oppressed by the ominousness of that. The question loomed, a palpable presence. Where was Ned? As the seconds passed — and the time was measured in seconds, not in minutes or hours — the answer imperceptibly took shape. Ned was in Newark Bay. The veil of unknowing was torn and the reality was there for everyone to see. A tragedy had occurred.

But no one in that stalwart family was acquainted with the word "tragedy." Things happened in life, and some were sad and some were glad and many were funny. But tragedy? Wouldn't that be some kind of overstatement? Wasn't that just a word you used in English literature classes? They simply didn't know how to act in this new presence, except to be brave, as brave as possible. As the horror grew plainer and plainer, their courage grew to meet it.

They made resolute conversation. They rolled around on the floor with the dogs. They answered the telephone and put the casseroles in the refrigerator, and when they ran out of room there, in the china closet. No one remembers who put dinner together that night, or if there was any dinner.

Ned pluckily went to school the next day, but John and Cubby stayed home. John remembers waking up and thinking, "If Dad's car's not here, he's dead," and walking slowly, very slowly, to the window. "That's it," he said to himself as he stared at the spot where the car should have been.

By now all the boys were beginning to feel a new and unaccustomed emotion: intense embarrassment. No one knew how to treat them anymore, and they didn't know how to answer when people told them how sorry they were. They weren't used to wholesale sympathy and universal attention.

Carl and Annie's brother, Arnold, arrived by car on Tuesday, and the two brothers went to see Annie. She told them she would sure like a drink, so they managed to sneak in a bottle of whiskey, and the three of them had a drink together. Arnie knew Annie had cancer, and believed that she knew it, although the truth in so many words had been kept from her. When they left she said, "Don't look back."

That evening, the evening of the second day, which passed no one can remember how, Annie called the house and asked to speak to each of her boys in turn. Carl, Arnie, and Sara were all there. As the boys remember that call, she was calm and reassuring. She didn't say anything about Ned. She told them she was fine and felt no pain. She asked them about school and sports, asked the older boys about the baby, asked how they were all getting along with Uncle Carl and Uncle Arnie, and said wasn't it neat that the uncles were there? She told all of them she loved them very much. She told them to stick together. She told them to go to bed.

And then she died.

Carl and Arnie got the message from the hospital after the boys were asleep. They had to be told the first thing in the morning that their mother was dead.

She had died in the arms of an Indian doctor, whose responsibility it then was to tell the family. "He was probably a Hindu," Carl said later. So it was on the kindness of strangers she depended in the end. It was to him she said, "No pain."

There was still no word of Ned.

4

The Accident

Accident: An inevitable occurrence due to the action of immutable natural laws.
> **Ambrose Bierce**
> *The Devil's Dictionary*

Back home on Cape Cod, I kept the radio and television on, waiting for word of my brother-in-law. I went to the Village News Store, morning and afternoon, to buy the New York and Boston papers as well as the local papers. It was important for me to find points of reference between my private nightmare and objective reality. If the accident was on the news broadcasts and in the papers, I couldn't have imagined it. I couldn't be crazy.

New Bedford Standard-Times
Monday, September 15:

TRAIN FALLS IN NEWARK BAY
COAST GUARD, OTHER CRAFT IN RESCUE TRY
100 ARE BELIEVED ON COMMUTER TRIP:
SOME PULLED OUT

Tuesday, September 16:

NEWARK TRAIN YIELDS 20 BODIES
COACH PULLED FROM WATERS

Wednesday, September 17:

27 BODIES ARE RECOVERED
ENGINEER'S HEART WEAK

New York Herald Tribune
Thursday, September 18:

DEATH TRAIN SALVAGERS RAISE
LEADING ENGINE

New York Times
Thursday, September 18:

WIFE OF VICTIM, MOTHER OF FOUR, DIES
MISSING EDITOR HAD SKIPPED EARLIER TRAIN
TO SHOP AND DO HOME CHORES

Boston Herald

Friday, September 19:

4 N.J. ORPHANS MAY MAKE HOME HERE
FATHER DIES IN TRAIN WRECK,
MOTHER OF CANCER

Cape Cod Standard-Times
Friday, September 19:

TRAGEDY TWICE HITS FAMILY OF BARNSTABLE
MAN'S SISTER

Indianapolis Star
Sunday, September 21:

BOY "MAN" OF FAMILY SINCE PARENTS' DEATH

The accompanying stories, creeping ever closer to the reality in Rumson and Barnstable, spelled out the disaster, but only a few of the details came through clearly to me at the time. In particular, I noted fine details about the timing. The train had left Bay Head, New Jersey, at 8:28, had stopped at Elizabeth at 9:57, and was due to arrive in Jersey City at 10:13. But the train must have left Elizabeth a minute or so late, because *the accident occurred at* 10:13. Those words leaped off the page and took a permanent place in my brain. That was within two minutes of when Carl had placed his call to Ned's office.

Even allowing for some fantastic Einsteinian time warp, that was close enough to simultaneous for me to think that something really weird had been going on there. I had not yet heard of Jung's word *synchronicity*, but when I encountered it many years later, I immediately recognized not only that I had experienced the phenomenon repeatedly, but, more importantly, that such experiences had significantly changed my life and those of many others.

The accident occurred at 10:13. Carl had placed his call to Ned's office within minutes of that time. Carl had never called Ned at his office before. Objective facts.

What happened simultaneously in the brain or the mind or the soul of Ned Willis seconds before he died, and in the brain/mind/soul of Carl as he headed for the telephone to call Ned? That *something* happened connecting the two events, I had no doubt. But what? And how?

I have puzzled over this and related questions ever since then. But acceptance that there was no way of knowing was part of the puzzle from the beginning. It had something to do with the very essence of time, in itself an impenetrable mystery. As the facts surrounding the accident emerged, I did not want to read all about it, but I forced myself to, in my need for objective correlatives.

The Jersey Central Railroad commuter train — consisting of two diesel locomotives, one riding deadhead behind the operating engine, and five passenger cars, each weighing 128 tons, with a total capacity of 375 persons — normally carried between 90 and 100 persons from New Jersey shore communities to lower Manhattan. On that Monday morning, 49 of the estimated 100 passengers were killed. The two locomotives and two of the passenger cars plunged immediately into the bay, after going through an open drawbridge, while one passenger car was left dangling from the bridge at a forty-five-degree angle. The remaining two cars stayed on the track. Railroad officials said they believed that the first two cars carried more passengers than any of the others. Several injured passengers were able to escape from the car that was left hanging before it, too, slipped into the water about two and a half hours after the first two cars went in. What happened was that the vertical-lift wooden drawbridge on a mile-long trestle had been opened to permit a sand boat to pass underneath. Although the tracks on the bridge were fitted with a precautionary device that is supposed to halt trains automatically when the bridge is open, and although there were three warning signals strung on the trestle approach – one a mile from the draw, another a quarter of a mile closer, and another 550 feet from the draw, all in working order according to the railroad – the train ignored all three and ripped through the automatic derailing device. The train might have escaped its watery plunge even then but for a caprice of timing. Normally, the huge concrete weights of the drawbridge block the track when the bridge is wide open, but they had started to rise as the bridge was being lowered into alignment with the trestle, and it was through this gap that the train hurtled.

Four of the six crewmen aboard the train died, including the engineer, Lloyd Wilburn, sixty-three, of Red Bank, New Jersey. Although Jersey Central President E. T. Moore called it an "unexplained accident," the attention of investigators gradually focused on Wilburn's health. He had had a complete physical examination, as required by Jersey Central regulations, on July 21, which showed him to be in top physical condition. But the autopsy report indicated that the engineer was a victim of heart disease and may have become ill at the controls. Testimony of witnesses later bore out the speculation that Wilburn surely would have slowed the train down (a tower man at the scene estimated the speed of the train as it hit the draw at thirty miles an hour, while surviving passengers thought it was sixty) to fifteen or twenty miles an hour if he had seen the "home light" two thousand feet from the open lift, which was showing red, indicating that the bridge was up. There was further testimony to the effect that the automatic derailer would surely have stopped the train if it had not been going at an abnormally high speed. The question then became: if the engineer had suffered a heart attack and was incapacitated, why didn't the fireman, who had train controls in front of him in the cab, apply the brakes? But forty-two-year-old Peter Andrew, himself a fully qualified engineer, was missing and presumed dead when the speculation turned on him. His body was found three days later.

It was established that the train was not equipped with a "dead man's control," such as is installed on New York subway trains, which is designed to halt a train immediately should the engineer release his grip on the controls. The reason, of course, that there was no dead man's control was that an auxiliary human being was in the cab.

After the lead engine was hoisted from the water by salvage crews, "available evidence" indicated that the brakes had not been applied until they had automatically gone on when the air hose was severed as the locomotive toppled into the bay.

A Jersey Central flagman who was in the fourth car and therefore survived said he had tested the train's air brakes before the run had started, and they had functioned properly. He had noticed nothing unusual until there was a sudden jolt and the fifteen or sixteen people in his car were thrown forward. He realized the train had been derailed and scrambled for the emergency cord, but before he could reach it, the car rocked to a halt, and he looked out to see the bay beneath him.

A baggage man in the fifth car said he had sat with Wilburn, the engineer, in Bay Head before the run started, and he had seemed to be in normal health at that time.

Beyond the facts about the mechanics of the train, the tracks, the bridge, the brakes, the warning devices, the pronouncements of railroad officials and medical examiners, and all the attempts at an official explanation, my attention was caught by a host of random details and observations of survivors, witnesses, and salvage crew members which I read in the newspaper accounts. Maybe somewhere in the morass of human reactions could be found better explanations.

Survivors told of swimming around in the sunken cars looking for a way out. "Suddenly we were in the water," said Rafael Leon, of Holmdel, New Jersey. "I started to pray I would drown quickly. My wife was beneath me in the water. I swam down and tried to find her but she had slipped down. I went back up to the surface of the water inside the coach. There was a window open...." Lloyd Nelson, a marine insurance claim agent, saw the open drawbridge, figured it might not close in time, and began opening a window. "By the time the car was in the water, I had the window open all the way. I swam to the surface and grabbed a hunk of piling that must have been knocked loose by the train. I floated on it for about three hundred yards until I was picked up.... I could see people all around me coming to the surface."

Two men in the third car (the one that dangled for two hours before falling), both with broken legs, somehow scrambled up the sharp incline of the car, out a window, and onto one of the pilings that supported the track.

Edward McCarthy, who owned the Elco Marina boating dock in Bayonne, was at dockside when he saw steam gushing from the water beneath the bridge. He immediately put out a small boat and in three trips brought back three bodies and nine survivors. "I tell you I never want to see anything like this again. It comes back to me how horrible it must have been for those people trapped under the water."

Patrick Corcoran, the bridge tender who pulled the switch that raised the drawbridge, watched helplessly as the train plunged into the water. "There was nothing I could do," he said. "I heard the rumble. I can't describe my feelings. I never saw anything like this in my life. I never saw such a mess in my life."

John H. Hawkins, the mayor of Shrewsbury, New Jersey, and a stockbroker, did a favor for a client on the morning of September 15. The client had requested that Mr. Hawkins bring $250,000 in negotiable securities into the city so he could arrange for a transfer of title. In order to comply with this request, Hawkins had to wait for the Monmouth County National Bank in Red Bank to open at eight-thirty, thus missing his regular commuter train and catching the later train instead. The securities were recovered intact from the wreckage, but Hawkins lost his life.

At the Bayonne morgue, Frank Jurtelowicz of Matawan, New Jersey, waited. He believed, but did not know for sure, that his wife, Veronica, and his four-month-old son, Paul, were on the death train.

I ploughed through it all, my brain cells collecting and storing the minutiae of the tragedy as if I were an official of the Interstate Commerce Commission or the New Jersey Public Utility Commission, both of which had instituted investigations into the disaster. I kept meticulous track of every detail, every surreal component, in order to anchor the reality of it in my head. If the drawbridge was 216 feet long, it must really be there. If the passenger cars weighed 128 tons each, they must be real.

I tried to imagine Ned opening a window ahead of time, like the quick-thinking marine insurance claim agent, and getting through it and waiting to be picked up on a piling. Or swimming frantically through the inrushing water and not finding an open window soon enough. Or finding a closed window under the water and not having the strength to break through it because he had no breath left. What thoughts must have gone through his head during those last moments? As time went by, each vignette was worse than the one before. Maybe he had mercifully been knocked unconscious at the initial impact and didn't have to deal consciously with the prospect of drowning. But he had had time to get that message through to Carl. Had he sent one to Annie, too? Had she also experienced some form of prescience or extrasensory perception that morning? If so, she never told anyone. Ned had sent a message to the person in the best position to *help*, I decided. That was the point. One of them.

And the body count grew steadily. From an estimated fifteen in the beginning, to forty a day later; from three bodies immediately recovered, to thirteen, to twenty-seven...

I searched the lists of the missing and the dead daily, learning the names, empathizing with the families. The name I was looking for did not appear until Sunday, September 21. Ned's body was found Saturday. His was the third to last to be recovered. He had been in the water for six days — one hundred and forty-four hours.

Those one hundred and forty-four hours were to be remembered in excruciating but various detail by the hundreds of people whose lives were touched — many changed forever — by that mysterious accident, people who would never stop asking questions for which there were no answers, try as the officials might to find them. What indeed was happening in the locomotive's cab as the train sped past the warning signals? If the engineer was dead or dying, where was the fireman? Why didn't he see the signals? Were they having an argument?

Was Peter Andrew trying to help Lloyd Wilburn in his death throes, both so deep in one emergency that they were oblivious to the other one about to overtake them? Why, oh why didn't one of them put on the brakes?

And what did all this have to do with the circumstances of various related lives: Ned wanting to be a scientist, Annie lying mortally ill in a New Jersey hospital, Carl having trouble with his career, me wondering what I was going to do next, our Matt having no brothers, Paul already missing his mother? And all the other multiform connections, an intricate cosmic spider web.

The answers, if there were any, were hidden in the mind of God.

A minute part of the answer (or the thousands of answers), from my groping perspective, was found in the simple fact that Annie and Ned were not separated for long. I believed they were together again somehow, that Ned had preceded her to the new whenever/wherever because she needed his help.

On this planet, another weekend had arrived. It was only six calendar days since we had savored the end of summer, but now those hours of innocent ignorance seemed more like six months or six somethings, unnamable and immeasurable, ago. Like the train, the world had hurtled off course.

By then, I had told Matt and Amy and Nelly as much as was known about what had happened. The children had no idea what this would mean for them, but they could tell by the way I was behaving and by the absence of their father that it was going to mean something.

How was it that a mother and a father could both just stop *being* all of a sudden? This sort of thing didn't happen very often, as far as they knew, but still, the fact that it *could* happen was as frightening as things can get.

What would happen next?

I collected all the articles without clipping them from the sheets of newspaper. I reread them once, as briefly as I could, one part of my mind denying what it was doing the whole time it was doing it. Two weeks later, just before the boys came to live with us, I stuffed the whole collection into a manila envelope with *Annie and Ned, Sept. 15-17, 1958* scrawled on it. I put the envelope on a high closet shelf, where no one looked for it or at it for the next twenty-three years.

When the time finally came to write it all down, every step of the exhumation of those old papers was slow and painful. First I had to find the manila envelope, under layers of other memories, good, bad, and indifferent. It was just where I had put it twenty-three years before, untouched, hard to lift from the awkward angle five feet above the top step of the kitchen stepladder. It wanted to stay where it was. Its molecules had blended with the molecules of the wooden shelf. I strained to lift it and nearly fell juggling it down the ladder, trying not to drop it and split its loosening seams. On the back of the envelope was written, in Carl's large block lettering, ARMAGEDDON IN RETROSPECT. I remembered that I had searched, that long ago September, through piles of disused manila envelopes with Carl's discarded story titles on them (they were his filing system) for one that seemed appropriate. And appropriate it was, especially nearly a quarter of a century after he had written it.

I put the envelope next to my Olympia extrawide-carriage typewriter and didn't touch it again for another three months. I had too much to do that summer, as I had all the other intervening summers. But the effort was begun. I knew the manila envelope was waiting for me in a place where I could not avoid it for long.

It was September again, of 1981, when I took the newspapers out of the ARMAGEDDON IN RETROSPECT envelope and read all of them, all the way through, for the first time since 1958. The process evoked the reality of the events described on the yellowing newsprint as if they had just happened. Then came the ritual of clipping the stories and the pictures and discarding the remainders of the old papers. As I did this, I found myself lingering over other items of the day: vacuum-pack coffee was 69 cents a pound; cooked hams, shank part, 39 cents a pound; the Board of Hospitals of New York City voted to provide birth control information and devices in city hospitals when medically necessary, a marked reversal of the ban on all birth control advice laid down previously; former president Harry Truman had taken a picture of Averell Harriman, then governor of New York, embracing District Attorney Frank Hogan, then running for the U.S. Senate, at a press conference at the Hotel Carlyle; a man could buy a Brooks Brothers Famous Own Make shirt for $8.00.

Why this concern for the trivia of the time? Simply so I could avoid settling down to telling the story I had gotten it into my head I had to tell. I needed these postdated news breaks in order to stick with it, the unfolding of the story as it was reported, day by slow day, during that fateful week so long ago. At last the papers were all clipped, and there it was: the tale of the deaths of Ned and Annie in a much diminished pile of yellowed paper.

As I began to write it down, to give it coherence at last, weeping as I wrote, my unruly mind expanded on every theme. "Car Dangles" — yes, but why wasn't Ned on that one? "Bridge Was Wooden" — yes, but it didn't matter whether the bridge was wooden or steel or brass or sterling silver, for that matter; it wasn't where it was supposed to be. "Bridge Had Device" — yes, but the device didn't work, didn't work, didn't work. "Little Warning" — yes, but isn't that always the way? "Seek Reasons" — don't we all?

And so, by the sheer repetition of the newspaper accounts, I ground into my mind the process by which my brother-in-law was transformed from an anxious husband, briefcase in hand, running to catch a late train, to a body picked up six days later in Newark Bay. The process by which his children became mine.

I could not get out of my head the thought of what it must have been like for twenty-nine-year-old Veronica Jurtelowicz, as her baby was snatched from her arms by the black, swirling current.

Some babies are given and some babies are taken. And that is simply the way it is.

5

September 17 Continued

**And all shall be well, and all shall
be well, and all manner of thing
shall be well.**
Juliana of Norwich
Revelations of Divine Love

In Barnstable, I put down the phone after that
nearly wordless conversation with Carl in New
Jersey, and just sat there staring into space, the
space beyond the kitchen window, out across
the golden-green salt marshes where the tide
rose and fell, rose and fell, exposing the mud
holes and then covering them up again. The
swamp.

I had to get busy. There were so many things
I had to do that, as Annie used to say, straight
I could not think. But first I had to let the
weight of what had happened sink in. There
needed to be a period of calm. Only the passage
of time could imprint on my consciousness the

truth of the matter, this quantum change in my life. Otherwise, I might wake up and find that it had all been a dream.

For my life had just changed as surely and irrevocably as if a space ship had dropped out of the sky and picked me up and deposited me on another planet.

Of course, the arrival of children is always like that, in a way. Once a child is born, nothing is ever the same. But a normal pregnancy is a more leisurely thing, a long, slow acclimatizing process. A *normal* mother mercifully is given a reasonable period of time to get used to the idea. But to acquire not one, not two, not three, but *four* half-grown children literally overnight — how does a mother get used to that idea? Well, by doing what needs to be done, the reasoning half of my brain told the half that was off wandering in space. Yes, but... But my nice, comfortable, anticipated, predeliberated, manageable family of five had just *exploded!* All those new sons! An avalanche of sons! My tidy little family of five had blown up into a wildly improbable gang of nine. Now was it possible even to refer to this new entity as a *family?* How was I supposed to know how to deal with such a freakish confabulation? Who, me? Over this rococo turn of events Carl and I had had no control whatsoever, yet we were clearly expected — by whom? how come? — to do whatever needed to be done.

Like Moses, I wanted to talk back. "You must have the wrong person. Don't you know I'm not very articulate? I'm not even a very good mother." But instead I got up and started moving. Like Columbus assigning his crew, I began to circumambulate the house, already seeing it as a vessel of exploration into the New World. It was necessary to deploy the crew. But the ship, until yesterday too big, was suddenly too small. Nelly would have to move in with Amy, never mind the five-year difference in age, so Paul could have the baby's room. Ned and John would have to share Matt's room, which was the biggest, because they were the biggest. Which meant that Matt could move into the alcove under the eaves above the kitchen, which he had always said he wanted anyhow. Cubby could have what had been the only spare room. This was a hideously flawed plan, as it turned out, from practically everyone's point of view. But it seemed reasonable at the time. How could I have known that Ned and John were mortal enemies, that Amy would terrorize Nelly unmercifully, that Paul could not be happy under any circumstances then, and that Matt would suffer from a bent ego as well as a bent back? The only one who came out ahead in the short run was Cubby, which was a special skill of his, as well as a powerful argument for children having their own rooms whenever possible.

It was not possible at that point. I paused in the single upstairs bathroom, centrally located amid the sprawling bedrooms — each one of which also served as a passageway to somewhere else — struck with an awful thought: how on earth can this one bathroom handle the traffic in the morning? They will never all be ready for school on time. My eye caught the four brand-new towel bars that had recently been installed. The last time I had given any thought to towel bars, I seemed to remember, there were only two: one for Matt, one for Amy, and a hook low down on the back of the door for Nelly. Nelly was to get a bar of her own when she got tall enough to reach it. I had no recollection of putting up the four new ones. Then, as I stood there in a room populated with specters from the future, already worrying about where to put their pajamas and how to get them to school on time, a wave of sweet familiarity drenched me. Of course! I had put the towel bars there for the refugees.

And then, with a marvelous healing swoop, it all fell into place. I *was* prepared. The refugees were finally coming. I knew who they were and where they were and what their names were and how it was they came to be refugees, and that in some unimaginable, incomprehensible, unexplainable way, they were meant to be my children. I hadn't needed thirty-six months of pregnancy to get ready for those four children. A scant two months, to the day, had done the job, with a hard labor at the end.

The sun had exploded in my head, hadn't it? And now I had four more sons. The cancer had grown and killed, but somehow out of it had come new life. They had all been through the fire, but now it was harnessed and life-giving.

Oh my God, said a voice in my head, coming back from the edge of the universe and the beginning of time, it is indeed true that You have most mysterious ways of doing things. Well, thank you, Lord. I had no idea what You were up to, but I'm glad to have been made ready, if this is the way You for Your own unfathomable reasons want things.

The final click of recognition came when I remembered that little Paul had in fact been born on Christmas Eve.

6

In Memoriam

Someday, after we have mastered the winds, the waves, the tides, and gravity, we will harness for God the energies of love: and then, for the second time in the history of the world, man will have discovered Fire!

Pierre Teilhard de Chardin

I did not go to New Jersey for Annie and Ned's memorial service, which was held in Rumson on Friday, September 19. Such a gesture would have meant nothing to them; in fact, it would have embarrassed Annie. She would have made a joke of it. "What are you doing here," I could imagine her saying, "when you ought to be home polishing the silver and putting your best satin pillowcases on the pillows and lace doilies on the backs of the chairs, because you have these fancy guests coming..." Annie would have wanted me to stay home and get their boys' new nest ready, even if what that really meant was locating enough old mended blankets to go around, and thanking God for space enough and towel bars.

But I took time out that day. I abandoned a multitude of half-finished projects begun in preparation for the arrival of the four boys, to go sit by the pond at the end of the meadow behind the barn, to look out over the salt marsh and the safe harbor beyond it, to grieve. I was beyond the stage of disbelief, the first stage in the mourning process. The facts had sunk in thoroughly, and now I believed. I needed to reflect on the lives that had just ended if the offspring of those lives were to be in my charge. If I fixed the personalities of the parents firmly in my mind, and the character of their lives together, it would surely help me to bring up their children.

Memories can help.

Annie and Ned had always lived in a world apart. Their reality was simply different from everyone else's in ways both profound and trivial, so much so that it seemed unreal to those around them. The roots of this dissimilarity to the rest of the world went far back and deep down. Annie was not like other little girls. She was taller, her hair was longer and more golden, her eyes were bigger and her eyelashes longer, and she was funnier.

"Funnier" is not an exact way of saying it (it's hard to be exact about her), as most little girls are not funny at all. But this girl, this myth of a girl with the stature of an angel, or at least of a princess, saw things from a different perspective than her contemporaries did, and this lent a whimsical enchantment to her perceptions and observations. She was not ha-ha-funny and she was not peculiar-funny, though she could be either at times. No, she was funny as no one in my memory or my recollection of literature had ever been: like a current of warm air out of nowhere on a frigid January day, or as if suddenly you looked up from your work and there was a peacock or a dolphin looking at you through the window! Her humor was always unexpected, but it was never (well, hardly ever) beyond the bounds of imagination. She would say something, and whoever heard it would think, "Oh! How strange and wonderful. I never thought of *that* before!" "Original" would be an unsatisfactory way of saying what she was, since everyone is original in one way or another. "Magical nonconformity" is better. The most beautiful child that anyone had ever seen, yet light-years from the stereotypical attractive child. There was absolutely nothing practical about her. Someone else always had to do the practical things – and gladly did for the privilege of being in her company. She drew and painted and sculpted, creating beautiful objects with apparent ease, all of it imprinted with her humor. If, as an adult, she had had more time and more money and fewer responsibilities, she might well have been a recognized artist, but by accident. The artistic spirit shone in her and through her, uncorrupted by ambition or competitiveness. Pure. Everything she did, she did for love.

Now all of this might have added up, one would think, to a combination guaranteed to make the other girls hate her – girls less beautiful, less amusing, less talented, and less able to avoid the messy mundanities of everyday life, or to transcend them. But no, surprise again. Everybody adored her. Because, on top of everything else, she was kind. She knew just what to say or do to make anyone feel better, no matter how unimportant that person might be to her or to anyone else, no matter what the problem might be, usually without her having the slightest idea what the problem *was*. She had no intellectual pretensions whatever. She never analyzed anything in her life. She simply existed in her own uniquely fanciful way, reacting with charm and grace to everything in the landscape, like a flower where one wouldn't have been expected to grow.

Her parents spoiled her a little. Who could help it? That had something to do with her inability, later, to deal with the harsh realities of the world. You can't expect a lily of the valley to do the dishes. You can't expect a bird of paradise to go shopping, or if it does, to remember what it went there for. Once, as a child, she saw a truckload of livestock being hauled down a street in Indianapolis on its way to the slaughterhouse, and she asked her father where they were going. He told her the nice people were taking the animals to another, grassier farm where they would be happier and have more to eat. Naturally, she believed it.

When the time came, Annie had suitors galore who would fall madly in love with her and then fall away when they found out how unusual she really was. She shed them for the irrelevancies they were with seemingly little effort. One irksome lad informed her that he was going to kiss her against her wishes.

"If you do, I'll throw up," she told him.

He did, and she did. And that was that.

I so admired this behavior for its utter efficiency. No one else I knew could have gotten rid of a distasteful boyfriend so naturally, so fast, so guilelessly.

Then along came Ned. Ned was up to her. She surprised him just enough, not too much. Ned had learned to walk downstairs on his hands at the University of Virginia, and managed to convince her that that was *all* he had learned there. That seemed an admirable accomplishment to Annie, one worth bragging about, an effective antidote for excessive egg-headedness. When Ned asked her to marry him, she couldn't think of a good reason why not, since she knew he was her soul mate. A high school friend of Annie's told me years later that she had never seen anyone so much in love as Annie was with Ned.

She wore sneakers to her wedding under an off-white satin gown embroidered with seed pearls and trimmed with antique lace (the same dress, shortened by six inches, that I later wore on my wedding day). She needed flat shoes because she was taller than Ned, and sneakers were the only white ones she could find.

It was immediately clear that neither of them could possibly have married anyone else. All the practical things that she couldn't or wouldn't do, Ned did. He cooked and cleaned and shopped, in between the never-ending frustration of negotiating with the outside world for money to live on, while she painted hearts and flowers and animals on the walls and the ceilings and the furniture and the dishes and anything else she could get her hands on, and kept scrapbooks of how the children grew. Ned was forty years ahead of his time. He would have been an ideal husband for an emancipated career-minded woman of the seventies or eighties, except that he wouldn't have liked her. Annie was forty years behind the times. The idea of a career never entered her head. "*Career? Me?*" she would have said, making it completely clear how silly a concept it would have been in her case. But she made a career of her boys, in terms of attention given and time spent. They were both exceptionally good parents – the most important thing they could have been under the circumstances, perhaps under any circumstances.

To an outside observer, their household arrangements seemed upside down, Annie frittering away her time in trivial pursuits while she should have been occupying herself with the everyday housekeeping chores that would have freed Ned to build a Successful Career singlemindedly, like every other ordinary, dull, driven man she knew – except her brothers. But she couldn't have stood him that way. As it turned out, she spent what time she had exactly as she should have, leaving for her sons, at the age of forty-five, a richer heritage than most mothers do at eighty-five. Her objets d'art are now treasured focal points in each of their households, while her immaculately preserved records of their infancy and early childhood travel from house to house, as the ark of the covenant followed the children of Israel out of the desert.

Many years later, I met the daughter of one of Annie's best friends. Tania has vivid memories of visits with her mother to the ramshackle house where Annie and Ned and the boys lived in Basking Ridge. "You wouldn't have believed it," Tania stated flatly. "Oh, yes I would," I said. For Tania it was like visiting Alice in Wonderland, and she treasured those visits. Annie, in long skirts long before they became sixties chic and with bare feet before the Kennedys made that O.K. too, was every child's dream of what a mother should be, and alas, so rarely was. "It was free-lance drawing all over the house," said Tania. "She didn't care. We could do anything."

Ned maintained the idyll. It was as if he had pledged himself to keep intact the gentle, rosy cloud Annie had always lived on, to never let it blow away, to never let her fall off it. And he delighted in the task. It was his mission. It made his scufflings with the workaday world worthwhile. How many men have a real live angel on a cloud to come home to? Annie was born to stay up there. Her whole life had prepared her to stay up there. Ned knew this about her and valued his ability to keep her there more than anything else. Any other ambitions he may have had were nothing in comparison.

So when they died that September, within thirty-six hours of each other, the awesome symmetry of their deaths seemed to be of a piece with the rest of their lives, a supernatural extension of their symbiosis, even a reasonable conclusion for them, where it could not have been anything but impossibly cruel for anyone else. When the love affair was over, it was over all at once. (Over? One couldn't help wondering.) Even those relatives who had brass tacks for brains felt that there was something transcendentally right about their concurrent deaths. It was agreed that Annie, well or ill, could not possibly have managed without Ned. And it was inconceivable that there could be another male on the planet with the precise combination of useful energy and zany romanticism, of sense and sensibility, that it took to be her husband. As for Ned, he would have tried heroically to bring up his boys alone, as indeed he had been preparing to do during the last few months of their lives. He knew how sick she was. But he would not have been able to do it with any degree of success. It would have been too much for him. The light would have gone out of his life. In fact, in the days when they were healthy and in high spirits, when no one could have guessed what was going to happen, those who loved them best actually said that neither of them could have lived with anyone else, or without the other, for more than a day.

Well, I reflected as I sat by the darkening pond on the day of the memorial service, they didn't have to, it turned out.

There was consolation in this for me and for everyone who cared. Difficult as it was to make the transition from thinking of them alive to thinking of them dead, a tender comfort rose, palpable as the evening mist that rose from the salt marsh. At least they weren't alone. At least they still had each other, somehow.

And this manifest comfort was there for the boys as well, although they were too young to give it a name or to understand what it was about their situation that was in some way all right, no matter how awful it was.

During the hour I sat there by the pond, my thoughts slowly evolved, changed from a confrontation with death to a confrontation with the lives ahead. Much life, many lives ahead.

Young lives had been broken. They needed to be mended. I would do what I could.

I had no idea where the energy was going to come from to do all the things that needed to be done, to meet the gaping emotional needs created by the double tragedy. But suddenly I did have the energy, and I found myself doing those things without even questioning the rightness of it. Many years went by before I could identify the source of the energy, could put a name to it. I had simply come face to face with *agape* – ultimate, unconditional love. This epiphany had no religious connotation at the time, as it came to have later. All I knew was that an inexplicable and extraordinary change had come over me as I sat by the pond and thought about Annie. It was Annie's true legacy to me, and made the rest of the legacy, all the messy, conditional, confusing, demanding, infuriating, inconvenient parts, not only bearable but embraceable. It was, in brief, a miracle. Only this time I hadn't imagined it. It was real.

7

Carrying On

Yet we have gone on living,
Living and partly living.
T. S. Eliot
Murder in the Cathedral

After the memorial service, it took another week for the packing up, the cleaning out, the planning, all the arrangements that had to be made in the wake of the deaths. Lawyers, insurance companies, creditors, real estate firms, employers, movers, and schools had to be called and dealt with. Insurance policies, birth certificates, marriage certificates, death certificates, Social Security documents, deeds of title, and all kinds of fine print testifying to this or that aspect of the lives just passed had to be located, organized, and presented to this or that official of this or that organization or agency or business or other body of individuals who had authority of one kind or another over those lives. The minutiae mercifully blotted out the immensity of what had happened for hours at a time. Advice on every possible aspect of the situation was sought and abundantly given. Many hot casseroles, meat loaves, cakes, and cookies were received and devoured. There was an outpouring of concern and tangible offers of help from friends, relatives, and strangers, near and far.

The piece of business with the most far-reaching consequences for the boys was a claim filed on their behalf against the Jersey Central Railroad, which never did produce a satisfactory explanation of how the accident had happened. It took a long time for the claim to be settled.

The house in Rumson was put up for sale. Clothes, furniture, household articles, and personal items were packed and decisions made about how to redistribute or dispose of them. Much of this was kept in big cardboard cartons, to be divided among the boys when they grew up. What was immediately useful was immediately used in the new household. The idea was to keep as much as possible of what was familiar to and beloved by the boys. The new family, having grown from five to nine, needed more stuff, and stuff it got, half a moving van and three carloads full. It took me weeks of sorting out, putting away, and saving up for later to take care of it all.

Letters poured in from people all over the country who wanted to help. An astonishingly large number of people wanted to give the boys homes, all of them. Most of the letters were addressed to Ned, as the oldest, some to Dear Children, some To Whom It May Concern. These letters, offering to take all or some combination of the boys, sadly received no answer. Ned was simply not up to it, and the uncles and aunts were too busy to pay attention. I didn't even see the letters until years later. It seemed to me they deserved to be acknowledged, but by then it was too late.

It was left to the boys to decide whether or not to go to school that week. Ned, still in the grip of denial the day after the accident, did and was mortified to find himself the center of attention. He didn't know how to answer all the questions the kids kept asking or how to acknowledge their sympathy. So he decided to stay home with John and Cubby for most of the following week. John and Cubby went back for a day toward the end of the week and were similarly horrified to have become a spectacle. There was a big goodbye event at John's school, where he was numb with sorrow and embarrassment: he said people looked at him as if he had a funny haircut.

It had said in the paper how brave and manly the Willis boys were, and so they did their best to live up to their new, unwanted reputations. They were indeed naturally brave — as children often have no other choice than to be in tragic circumstances — but to have this repeatedly and adamantly pointed out created unnatural expectations, a situation that they had to react to for its own sake. Somehow, these expectations of others undermined and diluted the natural grieving process, turned it into a public thing, leaving them little energy to nurse their sorrow privately. One of the results in later life was the strange amnesia that beset them all with regard to this period, and stretching back to the last days, weeks, and even months of their parents' lives.

The day finally came when it was time to move out. The great journey began twelve days after the train wreck, twelve days that no one can account for very coherently. On September 27, three carloads of boys, dogs, prized personal possessions, and what memories were left began moving in the direction of Barnstable, where I was doing my best to make room for it all. The moving van came later.

As for the trip itself, it was decided that Aunt Sara and Uncle Calvin, who had been on hand helping every day, would drive two of the boys and one of the dogs in their car, and that Carl would drive the old beige station wagon with the other two boys and the other dog. Uncle Arnie would drive separately in his car with another load of stuff.

But which two boys and which dog in which car?

The most intricate of deliberations went into solving this puzzle, which served, among other things, as a bridge from inchoate grief to the necessity of getting it all back together again, one way or another. Yogi, a large German shepherd, was John's dog, and a very dependent one at that, so clearly Yogi had to come with John. Sandy was Cubby's sheepdog mutt, and Cubby didn't want to be separated from Sandy any more than John did from Yogi, even for the seven hours it would take to drive from Rumson to Barnstable. But both John and Cubby wanted to come with Aunt Sara and Uncle Calvin, whom they knew much better than they knew Uncle Carl. Besides, they would be spending the rest of their lives with Uncle Carl and leaving Aunt Sara, whom they adored, forever. Ned was no problem. He wanted to go with Carl because he was old enough to be more interested in what was going to happen next, and he was up to the conversational requirements. It had become clear to Ned that there were now *two* heads of this family, and the two of them could talk things over, make plans, divide up responsibilities. And it seemed logical that where Ned rode was where Paul should be, because Ned was better at taking care of Paul than anyone else was. Also, Ned didn't have a dog.

But Paul's gear was already packed in Sara and Calvin's car, which was bigger, and it turned out to be impossible, or at least unnecessarily disagreeable, to get both Yogi and Sandy in that car along with Paul's things.

There was a standoff while everyone milled around and neighbors dropped in to say goodbye. Neither John nor Cubby would part with his dog. Finally John, the elder of the dog owners, got in Aunt Sara's car and whistled Yogi in beside him. Carl picked up Sandy and put him in the beige station wagon next to the driver's seat. The two back seats were occupied by Paul in his traveling crib and Ned. Cubby's choice was excruciating, but his options were limited. He climbed stoically into Sara's car next to John, trying not to look in the other car at Sandy, who had deduced that something wasn't going right and was whimpering mournfully. John's guilt reached the breaking point, but instead of moving Yogi out of Sara's car so Sandy could get in, he proceeded to repack

Paul so Cubby could go with Sandy. No one was in that much of a hurry anyway to say this final goodbye. Now John and Sara, not Ned, would be taking care of Paul, but never mind. Each boy got to ride with the right dog, which seemed the highest priority at the moment. John, of course, left the big box of disposable diapers in the car where Paul wasn't.

The person who heaved the most profound sigh of relief when they finally got under way was Carl. He hadn't picked any favorites, but he was glad that none of his passengers would have to have his diapers changed.

This chaotic departure, with its muddle of human and canine personalities, possessions, conflicting priorities, and divided loyalties was somehow symbolic and exemplary of the way life got in gear again for everybody. There were so many practical and urgent details to take care of that no one had the time to think about death anymore, at least for a while. That part was over. They would talk about it in the future and think about it privately when the mood overtook them, but it was no longer the main thing.

The role of the dogs in this turnaround was crucial from the beginning. They made it possible to organize. Yogi and Sandy had to be cared for and planned for. The integrity of their brotherhood had to be defended. They became a metaphor for the boys' own defenselessness, vulnerability, and need to stick together. In those early hours and days, when no one could speak the unspeakable, Sandy and Yogi became the rallying point. Thoroughly aware of their utter helplessness in determining what direction their lives would now take, Ned, John, and Cubby nonetheless held a private meeting the day after the accident and agreed on one nonnegotiable demand, no matter what the grown-ups said. Wherever they went, both dogs came too. To their credit, it never occurred to them that some of the grown-ups now mysteriously in charge of their destiny were seriously considering splitting the brothers up and had much less sensitivity for the dogs. Some deep instinct must have told them that their parents would never have permitted that, even from beyond the grave. But the boys saw clearly that the responsibility for keeping the dogs together was theirs.

That afternoon, presenting as formidable a united front as possible under the circumstances, they made their statement, disguised as a question. "Can the dogs come too? Can both dogs come? We won't go anywhere unless both dogs can come too."

The statement came out differently, depending on each boy's degree of vulnerability. With Ned, being the leader, it was an unconditional demand; with John it was half demand, half question; with Cubby it was a plea.

Uncle Carl looked at them in that mock-terrible way he had, his eyes red, remembering what it was like to be twelve and have a dog for your best friend, totally unable to imagine what it must be like to be twelve and have no parents. He remembered the dogs of his youth: Ogre and Satan and all the Spots and Blackies in between. He almost forgot the boys were there, nervously waiting for an answer, shifting from foot to foot. It was an affair of state, and they had had no training in these important matters. They had no small talk. Then he looked surprised, as if puzzled that they thought they had to worry about any other alternative.

"Well...what the hell. Of course," he said. "Damn the expense..."

The easy decision about the dogs served to underline the more important decision that had already been made by Carl and me at Barnstable Airport. At the time, none of the other relatives questioned Carl's assumption that he would take the boys back with him. Sara remembers pressure coming from somewhere for Calvin and herself to take Ned, but for a multitude of complicated reasons, that would not have been practical. Arnie's wife, Dot, though deeply caring and close to Annie, was not well then, so for the boys to go there was out of the question. Besides, Arnie and Dot already had five boys. The relatives in Indiana were not close enough to the situation even to be considered, and their children were all grown up. The nearby relatives went through the motions of deciding between this family and that, this location and that, but all the alternatives except going to Barnstable were almost automatically dismissed. Carl and I had a big enough house, were the right age, had children roughly the same ages as the boys, and were willing. And Carl was home all day. This last point was generally seen as an asset at the time, instead of the liability it turned out to be from Carl's perspective.

The other relatives didn't know about Carl's and my private reasons for knowing this was the right solution: the clairvoyant telephone call, my dreams and premonitions, Carl's promise to Annie on her deathbed. In unspoken accord, Carl and I thought it best not to talk about the more mystical aspects of our instantaneous willingness to take on four more children. Who would have believed us? The other relatives were known for their down-to-earth practicality and would have had no patience with such otherworldly imaginings and coincidences (as they would have described them). It was enough that there were so many strictly practical reasons for the boys to go to Barnstable. The relatives would help by sending money, especially during the early stages of the crisis, before the estates were administered and the Jersey Central made a settlement of some kind.

The other thing the relatives didn't know was how little money Carl and I had; if they had known, they might have vetoed the arrangement from the beginning. But we didn't think our precarious economic circumstances were worth dwelling on, since we expected that to change any day. Besides, Ned and Annie had always been broke. So what would be new? We felt it might even be beneficial for the boys to have a degree of continuity on this score.

What we didn't know was that the other relatives saw the four boys' staying together in Barnstable as a temporary expedient. Clearly, it was the only reasonable solution for the time being, but only Carl and I thought of it as a long-term commitment.

The truth is, none of them could imagine how it could possibly work out, Carl and I least

of all. Still, by means of mysterious conflu-
ences beyond our understanding or control, we
were committed.

8

Traveling Hopefully

There is an appointed time for everything.
And there is a time for every event under heaven.
Ecclesiastes 3:1

No one who set forth on that journey from New Jersey to Massachusetts can recall much about the trip itself. All John can remember is coming to the underpass on Route 6A, where years later Amy was to paint her series of angels, and thinking that there was something familiar about it. He and Annie had visited briefly three years before, so he had a vignette of the place in his memory. Cubby remembers a place in Buzzard's Bay shaped like a giant milk bottle, where they stopped for ice cream. He asked Carl at that place whether the kids on Cape Cod were nice. Carl said yes, they were nice, nice, very very nice.

The first carload to arrive was the one containing John and Paul and Yogi, driven in turns by Aunt Sara and Uncle Calvin. When it pulled into the driveway on Saturday afternoon, September 27, I was out in the barn, my reliable refuge, in an agony of readiness. I was trying to figure out how best to make use of every inch of available space when suddenly it had all begun. They were there. Fancy that! Big changes always seem sudden, no matter how expected they are. I wanted to scream, Not yet, not yet, I'm not ready! as I did when my babies were born. But I was ready.

John — who was so big now, I hadn't seen him since he was nine — leaped out of the car, and before shaking hands or hugging or kissing me (no one knew *what* to do), he urged this huge German shepherd into my arms. The trouble was, Yogi was almost as big as I was, up to my ears when he was on his hind legs, so there was some question as to who was holding whom. I tottered backward as he enthusiastically licked my face, and John caught me. The horn honked, and Yogi bounded off as Sara disentangled herself from the debris of travel. The baby was screaming, hot and wet and confused.

Since I hadn't been told about Yogi, naturally I asked who he was. Everyone laughed a little hysterically. The ice was broken.

Actually, there was no ice. With the immaculate precision characteristic of my kitchen, the refrigerator conked out. So, over warm lemonade and the familiar aroma of wet diapers, I was introduced to my new baby.

Paul couldn't help crying. He had been introduced to so many new people lately. He didn't understand this at all. Where were the ones who mattered? As clumsy new hands tried to pat him and comfort him and rearrange his clothing, he arched his back, stuck his fists in his eyes, and howled like a wild creature caught in a trap. John was the only one who could calm him down. John was better at it than anyone had given him credit for. Quietly, each big brother had learned how to care for his baby brother, changing him, rocking him, walking him, playing with him, tossing him in the air, talking him to sleep, their hearts breaking because he had been deprived so early of the parents they at least had gotten to know.

As John jounced and cooed Paul to sleep in the little room with hearts carved in the blue woodwork which Nelly had just vacated, Sara and I got acquainted. We had been through this terrible thing together, yet we had never met. We relived the whole tragedy, as people will as they work through grief. It's called "compulsive repetition" in psychological jargon, each of us revealing things about ourselves in the process. But it was more than just repetition. Sara could tell me much that I needed to know about my new sons, details about their development and attitudes and expectations that only someone close to them as they grew could have known, things that a mother has to know. And Sara could in turn be reassured about this new home to which she had just delivered her nephews. Everyone close to the family felt some of the responsibility for making the right decisions at the time, and that was a blessing. No one of them could have done it alone.

Still, in the background there were subliminal reservations on both sides. I knew that I and my home and my lifestyle were being sized up, but that was all right. I would have done the same myself had our situations been reversed. If I, in Sara's position, had had to make a judgment about the rightness of the decisions being made, I might have thought Sara just a jot too practical, just a tittle too precisely proper for these boys to have a happy home with her. I was subconsciously aware of Sara's quite opposite impressions of me, but I did not detect the seeds of her ultimate conviction that here was a ship not quite tight enough to stay afloat. At the time, things were in such a state of flux that no one could be sure of anything.

We all simply hoped for the best.

When Sara was reasonably sure that I was not going to keel over in a dead faint or depart for the Far East, she thought it best to leave, giving me some private time with my new children. She and Calvin left for Nantucket and a much needed respite from crisis.

Getting to know the boys was a sweet and shy procedure, and not a private one for very long. I felt like Emily in *Our Town,* wondering, as she contemplated the idea of spending the rest of her life with the young man who had just proposed to her in the ice cream parlor, what on earth they would talk about.

Whereupon Matt and Amy and Nelly came to the rescue, as children so often do and get so little credit for. The children have been rescuing each other and me in countless ways, large and small, ever since.

Children don't have the difficulties that adults do getting to know one another. They have difficulties, of course, but different ones, and later. The kids sized one another up very fast. They were intrigued by John, who at eleven and a half was already nearly six feet tall, could throw a ball, any ball, higher and farther than any of the local boys, looked like a Greek god (from Amy's perspective), and had an endless stream of stories to tell about the new mythical town of Rumson. They were enchanted by Paul, who had stopped crying, gone to sleep, and awakened in a better mood. He, too, seemed to want to get on with living.

There were tours of everything: every nook and cranny of the anfractuous house, the two attics, the cellar, the barn, and the yard. Then they spilled through the field down to the pond, down the lane to the harbor, through the village to the news store. All of this was a must on the first day, as far as John was concerned. He was a marvelously receptive guest and couldn't have been more enthusiastic. He loved everything, he said. Everyone wanted desperately to believe him. And no one really did. Reflecting on the day when it was over, I was happy, numb, grateful, and very proud of my children. The generosity of children, I thought as I drifted into a contented sleep, is a phenomenon too little noticed in a culture so obsessed with their failings and shortcomings and general intransigence.

The weekend passed more quickly than I would have thought possible. Matt and John were cordial, after the fashion of adolescents, as Matt moved his earthly goods from here to there in messy piles to make room for John's even messier mountains of athletic equipment. Once John was more or less randomly moved in, Matt bore him off proudly to meet his peers at the local playing field.

Meanwhile, Amy and Nelly took over Paul, swiftly mastering the art of diaper changing. Paul hadn't been so dry in six months. They lugged him upstairs and downstairs and all around the town, showing him off to their friends. All the little girls in the village from age four to eight wanted to take turns. Paul, being an adaptable baby from sheer necessity, forgot his misery. In between the shifts of eight-year-olds, I found space for some quiet time alone with him and found that we got along just fine after all. It wasn't love yet, but it was a start. Everyone was beginning to fall in love with everyone else.

I even baked cookies. It seemed like such a motherly thing to do. I had never made them before, so everyone was pleasantly surprised. Humppff, said my new self to my old, almost forgotten self, you had to be bonked in the head with a locomotive to turn into a mother, for God's sake! What was the matter with you before? Well, said the old self, begging for mercy, it was just never quite so focused before. Besides, I had other things on my mind, like trying to grow up. (This dialogue never ended. It threaded its way through the next quarter century.)

On Tuesday of the following week, into this cozy, sweet-smelling, floury, buttery scene, the other four arrived: Carl, Ned, Cubby, and Sandy. No one can remember why it took them so much longer to get there. Maybe the old car needed work. Maybe Carl had things to do in New York. Last-minute errands. In any case, my calendar records that they didn't arrive until three days after the first installment.

Remember? I said to myself. There's more. Remember? You've got this husband, too. I hadn't actually forgotten about Carl; I just hadn't had time to think about him. There had been so much else going on. Our life together, making babies and books and plans for books, seemed like a foreign country in some earlier century. Maybe it was gone forever. That would be a relief, in a perverse sort of way. Come back, come back, I said to myself, you seem to have another large dog in your kitchen.

Fortunately, or maybe it didn't matter, John had mentioned Sandy, though only by way of commenting that Yogi missed him.

"Who's Sandy?" I wanted to know.

"Yogi's brother."

"Oh."

But Sandy didn't look like a German shepherd to me. Sandy was a clumpy, whitish mop of a dog who couldn't see through his eyebrows.

Cubby was trying to introduce him, but it was no use. Sandy was already out the back door following Yogi, who was beside himself that Sandy was back in his life to help him bark at cars.

Now Cubby and I had the same problem that John and I had had. Do we shake hands? Do we hug and kiss? How do you greet a new mother, a new son you can barely remember having seen before? Well, you do everything all at once, as it turns out. Fumble with hands, hug with elbows in the way, kiss and fall down, burn the toast, let the water boil over, cry a little.

"You must be Aunt Jane," said Cubby appropriately.

"Cubby?" I said idiotically.

Meanwhile, Ned had lunged through the back door, carrying bags, bedding, miscellaneous bundles, and a bird. They hadn't told me about the bird. They called him Bird. Ned dropped all this stuff in a heap and picked me up. Ned was always picking people up. It was his way of showing affection, and also incidentally letting people know he was bigger than they. Then he put the bird on my head and said hello. It was nice to see him.

Next Carl straggled in, carrying more armloads of luggage. He was a haggard stranger.

How did he fit into all this, with his need for peace and quiet and, alternatively, for altogether different kinds of excitement? What of the two of us? How could our marriage, with its special needs, fit in? How would we ever catch up with each other after the cataclysmic events of the past twelve days? Or get back to that foreign country where we used to live? If either of us wanted to.

"You and I are past our dancing days," I said to him and he to me wordlessly as we embraced in the swirl of seven children.

But that wasn't true, as it turned out. There were twelve years of dancing days ahead, though not many would have recognized the dance.

9

Life Goes On

This supply of finer air had a name. It was called SOWF — the substance-of-we-feeling. The little trickle of SOWF that reached this place was the most precious thing they had.

Doris Lessing
Shikasta

The next day, Wednesday, October 1, some semblance of order and routine began slowly to emerge as the new family settled down to the serious business of living together. Cubby had to be enrolled in the fourth grade of Barnstable Elementary School and Ned in the ninth grade at Barnstable High School. John had already begun the sixth grade with Matt on Monday. Nelly started nursery school. An architect and a contractor, called on an emergency basis, came to discuss plans for enlarging the suddenly woefully inadequate kitchen. A man came to fix the dishwasher. A man came to fix the refrigerator. A man came to make sure the furnace would light without blowing up. It wouldn't, and, at great expense, he fixed it. A man came to patch the holes in the plaster in all the bedrooms. A man came to measure the upstairs bathroom for new linoleum. A man from the *Cape Cod Standard-Times* came for an interview. Friends and neighbors dropped by to ask what they could do.

Carl tried to get back to work. I didn't even try. I went shopping. The cashier's eyes bulged as she added up the contents of two overflowing grocery carts, and a total stranger asked if she could come to the party.

But the real action began when school was out at three-thirty. When the school bus brought Matt and Amy and John and Cubby home, it seemed that the entire fourth and sixth grades came, too. Everyone wanted to see the orphans up close. There wasn't much standing around and staring. It was more important for the fourth graders to feed the bird and for the sixth graders to stop the dog fight. John organized a touch football game, in which girls were allowed to play. He was an instant hero. This was his first political move, leading directly to the presidency of the sixth grade (elections

110

were the next week and he didn't even know it) and the captaincies of a wide variety of athletic teams in rapid succession.

Meanwhile, a splinter group of fourth graders found another idol; they got Ned to walk down to the beach with them to gather seaweed for the bird. Someone had the idea that birds liked seaweed. They found a sick seagull flopping around down there, so naturally they brought him home, wrapped in Ned's shirt. Another flourish of fourth graders headed down to the pond to look for a boat. They found a turtle and brought him home. Then the turtle had to be named, and an eyedropper had to be found to feed the sick seagull. Matt, the future doctor, found an eyedropper. Amy, the future artist, made a leash for the turtle. But since it was a snapping turtle, no one was brave enough to put it on. Finally, Carrie, from down King's Highway, achieved sainthood by getting the leash on the turtle.

It was time for more lemonade, but we were all out. Carl, having long since given up writing for the day, went to the store for more lemonade, also cookies and cupcakes. We were out of everything. I wanted to go with him; how else could we find a minute alone? We needed to have a real conversation about all this at some point, and there was no privacy anywhere. But it was really not safe for both of us to leave the property at the same time. Someone might drown or get bitten by a dog or a snapping turtle or a sick seagull.

Sure enough, by the time Carl got back with the lemonade and other goodies, mercurochrome and bandages had had to be applied to a victim of the beleaguered snapping turtle and to a little girl who had fallen down and scraped her knee just trying to keep up with things. The poor half-dead seagull, trying to avoid the samaritan with the eyedropper, had crept into the fireplace with a frantic flapping of wings, sending ashes everywhere. During this excitement, the turtle escaped into the dining room and was terrorizing Nelly, who had awakened from her nap and plonked downstairs to find out what was going on. As I scooped Nelly from the jaws of the turtle with one hand, trying to comfort the already bitten child with the other, I wondered whether it was possible to buy tetanus shots wholesale.

Nelly loved it. She clapped her hands and wondered whose birthday it was. Actually, it was someone's birthday; I just didn't know whose. It was *always* someone's birthday. This day it turned out to be Nelly's best friend Erin's. Quick, a birthday cake. Back to the store for a cake and two more community-sized cans of lemonade and more Band-Aids.

Outside, a giant dog fight was in progress. Everyone came. Yogi and Sandy, laying claim to their new territory, did not receive every neighborhood dog with equal civility. Papillon was O.K. (he was Yogi's new best friend), but Sounder and Sheik were not. Poor old Lulu, yearning for some action at the end of her leash at the orderly house next door, was too old to matter, but she could bark. One of the sixth-grade boys, aspiring to stardom in the new society coming into being at the corner of Scudder Lane and Main Street, intervened and got bitten. Now it really was necessary to get a tetanus shot. Off to Dr. Green's went Carl with three of the boys who'd been at the dog fight — just to be on the safe side. It was the first of countless trips to Dr. Green's for tetanus shots during the next five years.

And so the new amalgamated family life began. The tone of the new creation was firmly set within the first week. The big old house on the curving corner became a mecca for children and animals of all ages. Occasionally an intrepid stray adult would wander by, but for a time Carl and I more or less lost contact with our peer group. We almost forgot how to communicate with them. We made up our own language.

"Babble little booble-capper, tick-tock, tick-tock?" one of us would say to the other, meaning, "Have you seen Amy lately?"

"Ickle-squibble, no-no," the other would answer, meaning, "She's drawing on the living room wallpaper."

"Boo-boo boom-boom," meaning, "Paul has a mess in his pants."

"Urdle" — "I'll change him."

We understood each other perfectly. No one else did, but it didn't matter.

As the majority of the children approached adolescence, the pathetic minority of two achieved a certain wry juvenescence. It was the only way to survive.

Almost two years went by before I let myself remember in detail that early Monday morning in another age when I had dreamed of the peace and quiet that I thought I needed for some creative project of my own. In the meantime, I worked out my Doctrine of Infinitely Divisible Time. The reason, I reasoned, that mothers are perpetually dissatisfied with themselves for not being more creative is that they generally have no time that is not legitimately interruptible. Whatever they do, they do with the knowledge that they will be interrupted by something with a higher priority, and that thing will in turn be interrupted by something with an equally high or higher priority, and so on ad infinitum; so that eventually the original bit of a mother's "own time" is whittled away, utterly lost in a series of infinitely small particles of supreme importance, as in quantum physics. What you end up with is *no* time, as in 10^{-43} second, as split as a second can get, which is the sub-atomic physicists' way of saying the length of time it took for the Big Bang to occur. No time at all, as it turns out.

Had I been capable of generalizing amid all the confusion, I might have come to a conclusion that in fact it took me another twenty-seven years to formulate: the really important things happen in absolutely no time at all, like the conception of life, like death, like falling in love. So why do we worry so much about having no time? What started as a lament that I had so little ended in the surprising acknowledgment that I had all the time I needed for what really mattered.

Nevertheless, the lament went on. I spent years fruitlessly bemoaning the fact that I had no time to *do* anything. At the same time, nonetheless, regardless, irrespective, and in innocence of what was to come, I was obscurely grateful for it all, every hectic detail. As I sank, exhausted, into oblivion that first midnight of the new epoch, I thanked God for the endless, tiny, memorable *details* that had characterized, limited, encircled, circumscribed, and defined our new family's first few hours together. For it is the rich details of living that are paths to transcendence. These are tools, somehow, all these people and things and comings and goings and words and actions and "accidents." These are my tools, I thought, not even beginning to understand how such a motley collection of things and events could turn into tools. You can't just love in the abstract, any more than you can paint a picture in the air. No, you need five boys and two girls and one husband, three dogs, two cats, two birds, a turtle, lots and lots of friends, and much, much more, I suspected. I drifted into deep, blissful sleep that night, thankful that I had at last figured it out.

It? What was the *it* I was trying so hard to figure out?

It would be many years before this hypnagogic musing led me to a full understanding of the belief that has enthralled the world for twenty centuries, but which I had never been able to comprehend, try as I might. The Incarnation. The Body and the Blood. The whole concept of God taking on a human shape, and all the liturgy and ritual around that, had simply never made any sense to me. That was because,

I realized one wonderful day, it was so simple. For people with bodies, important things like love have to be embodied. That's all. God *had* to get embodied, or else people with bodies would never in a trillion years understand about love. So the Body and the Blood are for real. So *that's* what it's all about!

Out of such mundane material, religious sensibility is born. Carl's way of articulating the situation in which we found ourselves was this: "Hang on to your hats, we may end up miles from here."

And we did.

Part Two

Part Two

10

Ned

**If you'll believe in me, I'll believe
in you. Is that a bargain?
Lewis Carroll
*Through the Looking-Glass***

Edward Carmichael Willis, Jr., became the head
of his family at the age of fourteen.

No one aged fourteen is up to that, of course.
Ned did better than most. He also paid the
ritual price, is still paying, always will.

Ned is the only one of the boys who heard
nothing about the accident at school that day.
He was in the ninth grade, at a separate junior
high school. He went to a friend's house after
school and took his time getting home. When
he got there, all the premonitions of disaster
were in place: John and Cubby in tears, an
anxious babysitter, corroboration from his
father's office that his father could not be
found, and the news that both Uncle Carl and

Aunt Sara were on their way. After that Carl arrived, tried to calm everyone down, and left for the hospital. Ned went blank for approximately the next two weeks. The only thing he remembers in any detail is feeling responsible for the bills that were left unpaid. He took it upon himself to call the local grocery store to tell them that his father had died, and ask how much they owed. Carl, when he found this out, told Ned not to worry about that kind of thing. All the rest was the terror, denial, and embarrassment that beset them all.

He doesn't even remember how he got to the Cape. Strangely enough, neither Carl nor Cubby remember his being in the car on the trip north. All the molecules of Ned's mind and body must have blinked out simultaneously for a time. Certain mysteries persist.

But he blinked on again when he got there. Of the four boys, Ned was the only one who had spent any time to speak of in Barnstable. In August, just three weeks before the accident, he had been shipped from New Jersey for a week's visit. Carl and I hadn't known it then, but the truth was, Ned was a handful all by himself. His parents had needed a break. Annie had obliquely apologized in advance for whatever Ned might do.

"Is everything all *right?*" she had asked on the

phone once he had arrived, with a kind of mysteriousness in her tone that puzzled me at the time, but which I later recognized in my own voice when checking in with Ned's hosts, hostesses, and benefactors spread across continents.

It was on a Tuesday morning that I had picked up Ned at the bus station in Hyannis and brought him home. It had been a successful visit, in most respects, and a blessing in retrospect that the oldest brother already knew his way around a little and could reassure the younger ones when the need arose that they were not going to a terrible place. The memories were still fresh.

In fact, Ned had had a wonderful time. For years afterward there was an ungainly reddish-orange stain, like the first peep of daylight, on the kitchen ceiling to memorialize it. Ned always maintained that the ketchup bottle exploded all by itself. This was the essence of his constantly evolving scientific theory: generally, things explode if you give them just a little encouragement. He was only a few years behind the most advanced of the high-energy physicists who, since Einstein, had been telling the world that all matter carries within it the seeds of its own destruction. Ned must have figured out that the ketchup bottle would explode if you shook it vigorously with your thumb stoppering the top, thrust it ceilingward when no one was looking, and suddenly removed your thumb. If the person doing this happened to be six feet three inches tall, that would put the ketchup bottle in fairly close proximity to the ceiling, and the effect would be dazzling. Of course, it helped that the ketchup was one of those relics from the back of a kitchen cabinet, this one maybe from the forties and already fermenting when Ned found it.

Ned looked pleasantly amazed – his amazed look is also dazzling – and exuberantly cleaned up that portion of the ketchup which had landed on the walls, the fireplace, the counters, the refrigerator, the stove, the sink, the windows, and the floor. But what had squirted on the ceiling was harder to remove, even for someone six foot three and standing on a ladder. And so the shadow of its smile remained, a lingering memento into the next decade of Ned's volatile first visit.

That was just the way Ned was, even before tragedy ripped his family apart and he had more reason for being explosive. Yet his feigned innocence, his astonished "who, me?" look, was so convincing that he often escaped retribution for his scientific experiments. Not always, but often.

When Ned returned to Barnstable after the death of his parents, it seemed at first that he had changed. His more destructive tendencies went underground temporarily, while the outer Ned assumed the premature manliness that was to prove so costly to him in the long run. He was a "hurried child," not in the usual sense of a child pushed and shoved into overachievement by ambitious parents and a demanding society, but rather as a result of extraordinary events propelling him into an early maturity that couldn't be real or lasting simply because he was not ready for it. He took on the role of father right away and exercised it with the droll mixture of totalitarianism and protectiveness that has characterized his relationships with his brothers (and others) ever since. There was dignity and beauty in this, and it was very moving to watch, but it cost too much. He had to repress and curtail his own grieving process in order to meet the demands of his new position in life, in service to this fledgling unit, the Willis Brothers.

It was Ned who organized the brothers into as self-sufficient an entity as could be hoped for, so they could face the world unilaterally. It was he who interpreted the bewildering events to his brothers, he who negotiated with the near strangers who appeared from nowhere to take over their lives, he who disseminated information in both directions – from the brothers to the outside world and from the big world to the brothers. It was a heady place to be, and even though he had practically no control over anything, the ways in which he dealt with the illusion of control and the ways in which the illusion played back to him have shaped his character and destiny as definitively as anything that had happened to him earlier. Most of the life situations he subsequently got into contained within them the same combination of illusion and reality that set the tone of those early orphaned weeks. The price he paid was his memory. He forgot practically everything about his parents. He became amnesic about his early years.

One thing he did remember, with melancholy, was that he had never gotten along particularly well with his father. He was born while his father was away in World War II, so there never was a father-baby bonding for him. Ned Sr. was always more partial to the sons who had been born when he was home. Ned felt the discrimination keenly. So it was a mixture of grief and unconscious father-rivalry that motivated him to take his father's place so fast and so completely. The Oedipal implications of all this were clear, with the added twist that he never got to have his mother to himself because she died, too. The old days carried over to the new ones, in that Ned didn't get along very well with his new father, either. It was important for him always to be in confrontation with whoever had, or threatened to have, more authority than he. His rank in the new family then, after the original, quite remarkable switchover was accomplished, was slippery. Soon after having consolidated his position as chief organizer, he became chief agitator. If Ned couldn't find trouble, he made it.

It's not that the things Ned did were really terrible, but rather that they brimmed with terrible potential. What Einstein called "the holy curiosity of inquiry" Ned had in abundance. The key word was "curiosity," the key mode was Experiment. Everything Ned did, he did because he wanted to know what would happen next. How loud a noise would the thing (any thing) make? Would the door really come off its hinges? If so, how far would it fly? What would the expressions on the faces of people who saw it be like? He found his curiosity piqued and his imagination challenged everywhere he looked.

If you arranged some open safety pins point up under the slipcovers of the sofa cushions, and then figured out how to attach low-voltage electrodes to them, and then connected the electrodes to an extension cord, and then plugged in the extension cord, what would be the expression on John's face when he sat down on the sofa? The trouble was, the wrong person, some innocent friend of the family, was more likely to sit on the booby-trapped sofa, which was not according to Ned's plan. Then the whole thing would backfire, and Ned would be in terrible trouble. Again and again there would be the "who, me?" look and the whole routine.

Notwithstanding his antics — and especially because no one ever seemed to get really hurt — I fell in love with Ned. We formed an early and easy alliance. I sensed hostility toward him from Carl, and whatever good reasons Carl might have had for feeling that way, I thought it wasn't fair. I knew I was a pushover for Ned's charm, but what, I wanted to know when the issue arose, was wrong about being charmed by a charming person? Besides, there was always an element of humor in what he did. Most fourteen-year-olds had no sense of humor at all, or if they did, it was humor of the grossest, most obvious sort.

Ned's humor, in contrast, was outrageously broad but contained within it delicate subtleties that somehow broke up the outrageousness into manageable bits and pieces. Ned could, to use the most appropriate cliché, charm the bark off trees; then (to torture the cliché) he would grind it up and put it in your soup, so deliciously seasoned that you'd never know the difference. It was never poison bark. Ned always went an extra mile or two, again in a different sense than the usual meaning of that phrase, because it was always in some unexpected direction. He had endless energy for perpetrating complex activities and projects beyond the imaginative scope of most teenagers.

The "worst" thing Ned ever did is a case in point. On a walk down the lane one spring day about eight months after he came to live in Barnstable, he just happened to notice the tiny holes under the latches of doorknobs here and there, on the kind of doors you can lock and unlock by turning a small lever in the middle of the inside knob. He began to wonder how much space there might be on the other side of the little hole. What was the little hole for, anyway? Would there be enough space, for instance, to hold about half a teaspoon of gunpowder, a substance of which Ned just happened to have a little? The hole itself, as a matter of fact, looked exactly the right size to accommodate a small wick. Ned knew what a half teaspoon of gunpowder would do to an ordinary tin can, a Campbell's soup can, say: blow it about eight feet in the air and make a fairly satisfying loud noise. But it might be more interesting if the gunpowder was placed in something more enclosed, rounder, and shinier, and even more interesting if this object was also attached to something else of substance, like a door. The doorknob attached to the garage door of the eminent ear, nose, and throat specialist who lived down the lane seemed to fill the bill precisely. What effect, Ned asked himself, might an explosion of half a teaspoonful of gunpowder in Dr. Calvert's brass doorknob have on Dr. Calvert's garage door, not to mention Dr. Calvert's garage itself and the contents thereof. Once Ned started asking himself these questions, he had to find out. He had nothing against Dr. Calvert, had never met the sweet old man. Dr. Calvert had nothing to do with his doorknob's becoming a target.

At about the same time Ned was entertaining these speculations, a postcard addressed to him arrived in the mail from his oldest and best friend in New Jersey. I brought it in along with the rest of the mail and couldn't help noticing the message, since it was in large black scrawl on a starkly unornamental penny postcard: "Hope you got the fuses. Ammo on the way." It was signed with a skull and crossbones.

So, without going to any trouble at all to find out, I knew that Ned was up to something not very good.

About a week later, as I was taking the garbage out, I noticed a little pile of black powder right in the middle of the threshold of the barn, and near it, strewn about haphazardly, were some little pieces of cord about six inches long, some matches, and some candles. Close by was another postcard from Ned's friend in New Jersey, saying, "You owe me $6.95." Skull and crossbones.

Whatever it is, I thought, he's about to do it.

Now, a disinterested observer might wonder why I did not, at this point, sound some sort of alarm or call upon whatever forces of law and order were at my command. But it must be remembered that there were no disinterested observers in those days, and that causes for alarm were so rampant that a little pile of gunpowder, etc., on the barn floor was not all that much more significant than anything else. Besides, I did not have time to think about it. The reason I was in such a hurry on that particular day was that I had to get the mess from Matt's birthday party cleaned up before Paul and Nelly woke up from their naps and resumed their strategies for mutual extermination. (More on this later.)

The point is, there was no time in between catastrophes already in process to deal with future eventualities, the dimensions of which were not at all clear.

But the dimensions of this particular catastrophe became all too clear all too soon. I *had* heard an explosion, but didn't connect it to the evidence of Ned's planned explosion. We usually dismiss loud noises — bangs, screeching brakes, even single screams — as somebody else's problem. When the policeman knocked on the back door, I was not the least surprised to see him. I had, so to speak, been expecting him. And when he asked whether it was possible that someone in the house might be responsible for the explosion that had a few hours earlier blown the door off Dr. Calvert's garage and shattered the windows and flattened the shrubbery in the vicinity, I replied that it was not only possible, it was probable.

This candid response, seconded by Carl, who always emerged from his study when the cops came, earned us no respect from the assembled multitude of kids, who, having heard the explosion and seen the cops, knew where to congregate. But Ned, his eyes never more lamblike, said he had no idea what everyone was talking about.

This was flabbergasting. The evidence was

simply overwhelming: the postcards, the gunpowder, the fuses. None of which I had mentioned yet, thinking surely I wouldn't have to, since Ned would of course confess immediately.

Think again, I said to myself. This is not going to be as simple as you think.

Another piece of incontrovertible evidence was that Ned and his new best friend, Ken, a fellow conspirator in most of Ned's more sophisticated projects, had been seen walking down the lane about a half hour before the blast and strolling nonchalantly back past the scene of the crime approximately half an hour afterward. Ken had quickly split for home, but that didn't fool anyone.

The explosion had been heard by everyone in roughly a two-mile radius, startling people as far away as the Village News Store. It had been a successful experiment.

In spite of all the clues pointing in his direction, Ned's consistent response was flat denial. The other kids, observing the mounting case against him, were visibly surprised that he stuck to his story so stubbornly. But they remained fiercely loyal. Tension grew as everyone under fifteen presented a united front against the pitiable man over thirty. It was Them versus Us. If Ned said he didn't do it, then he didn't do it, from a kid's-eye view. Even though everyone knew perfectly well that he *had* done it.

Parents are well known to be traitors. But these children had never thought their parents capable of such treachery, parents so perfidious that they would actually turn an innocent child of their very own over to the cops. Outrage! Worse, an innocent orphan child! Hadn't Ned been through enough already?

Carl and I were confounded. The police had left us to our own devices to get the truth out of this patent delinquent. No charges were pressed, chiefly because the victims were sympathetic to the situation of the poor orphans. We had two options. One was to believe Ned, in spite of all the evidence to the contrary, and go on as if nothing had happened. This would set a horrendous precedent. All the children would grow up thinking that they could do destructive things for fun, lie about it, and get away with it. It would mean, we knew in our bones, that we would never know for sure whether the kids were telling the truth or lying, and furthermore that we had capitulated on the issue of whether it mattered. This seemed an untenable position for parents to be in.

Equally untenable, at that point, was the notion that Ned could be persuaded to tell the truth. Three days after the event, he was still so firmly embedded in his lie that it seemed as though we had lost him forever. Tensions and antagonisms mounted, filling every nook and cranny of the collective consciousness, until it seemed as though the lie had acquired a personality of its own, a personality to be either defended or attacked. Ned grew distant and cold. Carl and I felt defeated and helpless.

The impasse went on for a week. It was a case for a family therapist, or some form of psychological help, but Carl and I were somewhere between ignorant and distrustful of such solutions in those days. There was no one on the Cape we knew of to whom we could turn.

Finally, Carl decided he couldn't stand it any longer. It was getting boring, a state of affairs never to be tolerated for long. He made his master power play. It was immensely effective, since it was the first real confrontation between the two of them. He sat Ned down at the kitchen table, with the usual audience of kids gathered around, and said, "All right. We're prepared to believe you. We will believe you, and there will not be another word about this, if. . ."

They were staring at each other across thirty-six inches of pine table, Ned's blue eyes honest and unflinching, Carl's bloodshot and weary.

". . . if you will give me your word of honor that you didn't do it."

Everyone stopped breathing. You could have heard the proverbial feather drop. To the unspeakable relief of the audience, Ned averted his eyes. He just sat there, pale, staring now at the table. He didn't say a word. The children cheered. I sagged. Carl got up and, for the first time in this house, hugged Ned. I hugged Ned, Ned's eyes filled with tears, and he had to leave the room to keep from breaking down. But the tension was gone, like the air from a popped balloon. Everything was all right again, and everyone knew it. Quiet jubilation filled the house as the kids fanned out, each thinking of some way to make Ned feel better. The episode had been very hard on Ned, who had no idea why he had behaved as he had at any point during the entire affair.

A deeper understanding of the whole thing took months, even years, to work through. Without professional help, we worked at it in bits and pieces, trying to get Ned to understand his motivation in lying, in sticking to his lie so stubbornly for so long, and to understand why he needed to blow up Dr. Calvert's garage door in the first place.

But the details of retribution were easy after that. Ned had to confess to the Calverts, apologize, and pay for the damage. The Calverts, to their credit, held no grudge.

To me, thinking of the family as a whole, the most important thing was that the right precedent had been set when we had come so close to doing it wrong. I was struck anew by the importance of the decisions that parents have to make. The danger to all the young people watching the drama as it unfolded had been much more than the potential danger to Dr. Calvert's second car and summer furniture. It was a close call, but everyone had won. Thenceforth it was understood that the fun of blowing up other people's property is not worth the inevitable fallout and, more importantly, that it is not necessary to lie — in the occasional event of having forgotten the first point — in order to preserve one's dignity or to retain the love of one's parents. It had been proved beyond a shadow of a doubt that lying was a lot more trouble than it was worth.

The adventure was a turning point in the dynamics of the group. It brought us together in interesting new ways and provided for each generation a better understanding of the foibles and tribulations of the other. Its lessons were never forgotten.

They say that the oldest child has the worst of it in most families, suffering from all the mistakes his or her parents don't have enough experience to avoid. Ned had two sets of neophyte parents to contend with. It struck me in later years, when the mission was completed, as something of a miracle that Ned grew up at all. An ongoing miracle.

11

John

**It has to be over
Before you can say
"That's the best time
I ever had."
From a song by John**

In the beginning everyone thought John would be the easiest. According to all received accounts, he was the best adjusted of the boys, the most outgoing, the most popular, the most polite. At the age of eleven, Success with a capital S was his. He was the best student (all A's), the best athlete (captain of every team in sight), and the least trouble around the house — partly because he was rarely there. He shared none of Ned's nerve-racking destructive tendencies.

Since John had so much going for him, one would have thought that his care would have been a breeze. Isn't it every parent's dream to have a kid who is absolutely wonderful at everything he does? Who is loved and admired by everyone and never feels left out? Who is ever considerate of other people's feelings? All of this certainly did have its advantages, especially in contrast to Ned, who was always up to something suspicious. But about six months into the new family scene, I realized I had no idea who John really was. The trouble was, there was no time to talk to him, ever.

John's modus operandi, when he came home from school, was to get on the telephone. He never stopped en route from door to phone.

"Hi ya," he'd say once he got on the line.

The sixth grader on the other end must have responded equally loquaciously.

"Whatcha doing?" John would continue. "C'mon over. No. Can't. Yeh. Bye."

An approximation of this stimulating conversation would be repeated some seven or eight times, and thus was the master plan elaborated for some event, usually athletic. Then zip, zip, a light breeze from the slamming back door would mark his departure, and before I could remember what it was I wanted to tell him, the touch football game was in full sweat in the side yard.

If you're president of everything and captain of everything and everyone's best friend, it's hard to keep on top of it all. It was difficult to get his attention, since there were so many important things occupying it at all times. If he happened to be involved – in passing – with the family, on Christmas morning or at Thanksgiving dinner, say, the phone would ring. It would always be for John, and off he'd go, zip, zip.

John was a hurried child in an entirely different way than Ned was. All his frenetic activity, his ceaseless socializing, was his defense against the terrible thing that had happened to him. He was the most susceptible of all the boys to the cruel machismo notion that brave little boys don't cry. But if both your parents die when you're eleven, how can you help crying? One way is to keep so busy that you don't have time to think about it. And because John was so busy guarding himself against the reality of what happened, he also had to keep the new reality, the new family, emotionally distant. It was easier to keep running and jumping, dodging, catching, and throwing balls, zigging here and zagging there, getting the wind knocked out of him at least three times a day, than to admit he had a new family. If he admitted that he had a new family, then he'd have to admit that the old one was gone, and that was the one thing he couldn't do, because he might cry.

Standing in the draft from the back door that

his last exit had created, I would sometimes think that all this gross motor activity was John's way of biding time until the day the phone would ring and it would be his father saying, "Hey, beanhead, come home now. Mom's out of the hospital and I just made a million with the new adhesives magazine... Tell Ned and Cubble it's time to come home now, too... I'm proud of the way you've handled this thing, John." Or something like that. Who could guess what his fantasies might be? I knew he was suffering under the cover of his perpetual motion, but I didn't know how to help him with it. The barriers he had built were too well made, too plausible. He always said thank you after every meal.

I knew how perverse it was to be heartbroken because an eleven-year-old said thank you for dinner. Most mothers I knew would have traded something of considerable value to hear those words just once. But I knew also that it was John's way of saying, "Don't get too close to me. Don't pretend you're my mother when you're not. My mother is not really dead, she's just sick, and I'm just here until she gets well. And thank you very much for the delicious dinner in the meantime." John's elaborate thank-yous let everyone know that he was only a guest, not a member of the family.

142

Not being able to find some reasonable middle ground with either of my two new big boys was unsettling. If, for starters, Ned would only have been a little more considerate of the feelings and property of others, and John a little less so, it might have been possible to find a firmer footing in the crazy house that life had become. But no. Neither personality seemed able to express itself in less than wild extremes. I honestly didn't know which I hoped for more, for Ned to do something good or for John to do something bad. The whole notion of setting standards for teenage and preteenage behavior was stood on its head.

Meanwhile, I mourned and puzzled over the suffering, polite, successful young stranger in our midst — until one Saturday afternoon, early in the baseball season, when there was the beginning of a breakthrough.

John was feeling queasy that day. He was going to pitch for his Little League team for the first time, and the new responsibility weighed heavily on him. As I drove into Hyannis with him beside me, I was thinking: this will make my six hundredth hour sitting on that bench; I wonder when he's going to notice — when John suddenly said in a strangled voice that he felt like throwing up. This was so close to being impolite that he could hardly get out the words. I pulled over. Fortunately, there was a small wooded area just before the baseball diamond. John plunged frantically into the woods so as not to be seen by his teammates. Some inspiration made me follow. His sickness was urgent. He vomited prodigiously; there seemed to be no end to it. Because he was in such desperate need of it and because he was in no condition to protest − "Don't mind me, I'm having a wonderful time," he would have said if he could − I held his head. That had always seemed to me as a child the ultimately comforting thing a person could do for another in that situation, so it had become a reflex when my own children got sick. I held his head firmly, as in his extremity he gave himself up utterly to a helping hand.

When it was over, we both wiped our sweating brows.

"Thank you," he said.

My heart leaped as I heard the different tone of this thank-you. He was not just being polite. It was a new kind of gratitude. We both laughed at the irony, standing in the spewed out wreckage of his lunch.

"I'm not really a very good pitcher," he said, grinning.

"You'll be fine," I said.

And he was.

That was the beginning of a genuine dialogue with John, sporadic and halting at first, but better and better as it matured. The process of expanding trust took several more months to develop and reached a culmination one November evening the following fall.

I was in the kitchen finishing the dinner dishes, about to collapse after another day of infinite variety encapsulated in the same old routines. John strolled into the kitchen, making me suspicious at once. Why wasn't he running? He must be thinking about something.

"Here. If you want to read this, you can."

He handed me a messily typed ten-page report that was due the following day. I knew about it because he had been complaining bitterly for a week that school work was interfering with his social and athletic schedule. He had been dispensing clues that something new was going on in his life. I understood by then how to interpret his veiled requests for help, and knew that what he was really saying was "Please read this. I want you to read it. Please."

The temptation to say "Not now, John, I'm just too tired" was almost irresistible. I watched his back as he beat a characteristic strategic retreat. He hadn't given me a chance to reply, but had just left the report lying on the kitchen table. He had never done such a thing before, had never asked for help on any school project, not even for spelling. It would have meant getting too close. He didn't want to intrude on his hosts.

There must be something special about this paper, I thought. I stifled my fatigue, dried my wet hands, and sat down to read it. I could hear John lifting weights in his room. That's what he did when he was nervous, also when he wasn't.

Before I had finished the first paragraph, my fatigue was gone. It dawned on me that this was one of those small miracles of good timing. Thank God I had not begged off. If I had, he might have taken it back and been overcome by shyness again. He might never have given me, or any of us, another chance to know how much he really cared. By reading this seventh-grade report on "How I Spent My Summer," I discovered a depth and tenderness in John that he had never dared to show. He did acknowledge his new family. He loved them; he just didn't know how to go about saying so. He didn't even know how to say he couldn't say it. There was so much he didn't understand about his loss and his response to it and to his new family. But he was struggling to get it all in perspective.

He might not have been able to say what he

was feeling (because he might cry) but *he could write it*. Thus, incidentally, came the realization that John was a born writer. I had never even suspected this dimension of him, since he had kept so crazily busy trying to keep it from himself. Now that it had been shown to me so vividly, the shock of recognition was staggering. Of course. A kindred spirit. Hadn't I been trying to do the same thing myself all these years? Of all the hidden gifts to emerge from their changed life, this was the most surprising. As Elizabeth Barrett Browning wrote:

> God answers sharp and sudden on some
>   prayers,
> And thrusts the thing we have prayed for
>   in our face,
> A gauntlet with a gift in 't.

The report was beautifully written. It was an account not of the past summer only, but of the past two summers, and of the contrasts between them. He wrote of the last months of his old family, the deaths of his parents, the move to Cape Cod, and the strange numbness that had followed. Until recently. Sometime during the past few months had come a thawing, then a turnaround and a new beginning.

"And then I was given a wonderful new family. . . ." He described us all with subtlety and warmth, sensitivity and humor. He didn't leave out the less than wonderful parts, or even the downright bad parts, but he included them with generosity. It was filled with powerful insights and a sense for delicate shifts of emotion. Scenes that I could have sworn he had not noticed at all were brilliantly evoked. The feeling that came off the pages was acceptance after struggle, thankfulness, even joy.

He was candid about the pitched battle he had had with himself before he could sincerely feel that way. John had always suspected himself of hypocrisy. He objected to starting a letter with "Dear" because he often didn't think of the person to whom he was writing the letter as particularly dear. Similarly, he couldn't comfortably sign it "Sincerely" because he doubted his sincerity about whatever was in the letter — even if it was only a thank-you note for a scarf for Christmas. What if he didn't really *like* the scarf? Then what? Poor John. He reminded me of the Cowardly Lion and the heartless Scarecrow and the stupid Tin Woodman all rolled up into one, bemoaning the lack of that which he was in the process of exemplifying. "See, I have no heart," he was saying as he handed it to me.

I sat at the kitchen table with tears streaming

down my face, knowing what it had cost John to show me that. He had finally decided to join the family.

About half an hour later he came downstairs, having lifted all the weights he could, looking embarrassed. I had pulled myself together by then, but I knew he knew I had been crying, and he knew I knew he knew. So what was the use of pretending? We laughed and cried at the same time. I told him I really needed to know that, and he said he did too, both of us forgetting if we were talking about some special thing in the report or the report as a whole. Neither of us was sure what this excess of feeling was all about, but it sure felt good.

"The point is," I said, knowing it wasn't the point at all, just one of them, "you can really *write!*"

The point was that we had found out we loved each other.

The episode marked the beginning of John's career as a writer. Later that night, I told Carl about the luminous exchange, and he asked to read the piece. This gave Carl and John something in common that they had not had before. The mutual admiration thus engendered grew as John grew, not without interruption, but to the benefit and credit of them both. John had not only joined the family, he had adopted

Carl as a role model, superimposed over the image of his own inventive father.

Adoption or, as in this case, guardianship, is not a one-way street. As it turns out, parents and children have to adopt each other.

One fascinating by-product of John's new introspection was that very early on he decided he was too old. This development took a few years, but at about the age of eighteen, he started mourning his lost youth, and he hasn't stopped since. He memorialized his nostalgia most vividly in a song entitled "Canopy Bed":

> Ain't it a shame it can't stay the same,
> Just some rusty springs to show
> From the happiest times we spent
> sipping wine
> In the woods such a long time ago.

Other pieces of his work reveal a yearning for the carefree days of early boyhood, ended for him so prematurely, so heartbreakingly abruptly: Paradise Lost. At age twenty-one, the picture of youth and health, John thought he was over the hill. The thought of advancing age continues to hold more terror for him than for most of his contemporaries, because he has learned that by the time you turn forty, you might die.

He's thirty-nine now, and only about halfway up the hill.

John and I actually climbed a very steep hill — almost a mountain — together once, on the spur of the moment. We were in Jamaica, at a turning point in both our lives, and suddenly it seemed reasonable to climb straight up the side of the hill that was between us and where we wanted to go, rather than hike around it. So up we went, panting and giggling like children, muddy and scratched and sweating by the time we got to the top. John had to help me over the steepest parts, but we did get there. We got to the top. It only took an hour.

12

Cubby

If I had the wings of an angel...
Anonymous

Cubby. Cubber. Cubble-Woo? Cubbler.

You can make up your own if you want.

When Cubby was born, they named him Caleb Jonathan Willis.

Then they looked again. He wasn't a Caleb, and he wasn't a Jonathan. He was a bear cub. The reason he was a bear cub was that he was the most angelic-looking baby anyone had ever seen. Snapshots taken of Ned and John and Cubby all heaped up together in a big armchair when Cubby was only a few months old show two squirmy little boys with runny noses who would rather be outside playing, and on their laps something that looks as though it just got taken out of a big shiny gift box from Bloomingdale's. He was just too beautiful to be real. People looking at the photograph wonder why the two normal-looking little boys are playing with such a big doll. So naturally they named him Cubby. Something had to be done to counteract this angelic perfection.

It worked. He's real.

When the boys first came to their new home, everyone assumed Cubby would be the most difficult, because he was the youngest who was not actually a baby. He had been the baby of the family for a long time and was his father's favorite — or rather his father's most recent favorite. Annie tried to balance this out by not having favorites, but it didn't work. The family pattern was that each new baby was a favorite when he was new, and Cubby had simply stayed new longer. His status as the youngest had remained uncontested for nearly eight years, both Ned and John had been displaced from that position after three and two years respectively. So Cubby was, if the truth be told, spoiled, after the manner of the baby of the family.

Ned Sr. used to drive with Cubby in his lap, a hair-raising habit seen from the perspective of today's seat-belt awareness. Big Ned was told repeatedly that it was a dangerous and dumb thing to do, but he paid no attention and went everywhere with his baby in his lap, like a daddy kangaroo who had grown a pouch. Ned took Cubby everywhere he went whenever he could, especially during the last months of his life, while young Ned was off getting into trouble, John was playing ball of one kind or another, and Annie was busy with the new baby. This made for a closer than ordinary tie between father and son, and so it was logical to think that Cubby would be harder hit than his brothers and consequently harder to handle.

The exact opposite turned out to be true. All the special attention had given him an extraordinary sense of security. Cubby had basic trust to the nth degree, the most important first stage of healthy personality development. He was so secure that, given any reasonable opportunity to believe that a person or a situation was to be trusted, he would go for it. But he was also a vulnerable nine-year-old whose most dependable objects of trust had suddenly and cruelly been taken away. What he had to do to survive, then, was to transfer his trustfulness to the new situation as quickly as possible.

That is exactly what he did. Being an extremely practical little boy who wanted to get on with the process of growing up as efficiently as possible, he did it very fast. The process by which he transferred his allegiance took place in a little less than two weeks — in contrast to Ned, who took the better part of a year, and

John, who spent well over a year at it.

At first Cubby was shy, as they all were, each in his own way, and stuck pretty close to his big brothers. His first incentive for prying loose from them was Amy. The very concept of girls was an oddity for this all-male gang. Although there had been episodes of puppy love from time to time, none of the boys had really had much experience of girls. Now, as if they didn't have enough to cope with already, there were two girls in their immediate family to whom they were supposed to relate as if they were sisters. Cubby had an advantage over his older brothers in that Amy was almost exactly his own age — a peer sister.

Amy was a bigwig of sorts, being beautiful and talented and fairly sophisticated for eight (really almost nine). Amy knew a good thing when she saw it, and Cubby qualified. Amy was almost immediately transported to heaven. She got to take her handsome new cousin/brother with her to his first day in his new fourth grade, got to introduce him to the other boys and girls, got to explain to anyone who was interested — and everyone was — how he came to be called Cubby, got to point out the dashing scar on his neck where he had had a tracheotomy when he was two and explain that that's where his other head used to grow, got to discuss at length, with living proof in the same room, the incredible things that had happened to the family. And then she got to put her arm protectively around him, little mother that she had become overnight, and take this enchanting creature home with her. Amy and Cubby, in short, found themselves elevated to stardom, and they reflected each other's glory mightily in the firmament of Barnstable Elementary School's fourth grade.

There was no competitiveness between them. There was enough of that to go around among the male members of the family: Ned competing with John, John competing with Matt, and Matt, of necessity, competing with everyone in sight. For Cubby, Amy was a blessed relief from all this rivalry business. Being a girl, she was no threat − to him, anyway. It was nice to have someone his own age to play with. Years later, I found Amy's diary from that year. On every page was the same notation: "After school Cubby and me played, and..." It made for tedious reading, but it said worlds about their friendship.

I quickly and gratefully realized that Cubby was not going to be any problem at all, and so we both felt the shyness recede as we relaxed into an easygoing relationship. Cubby would come to the kitchen after dinner, when everyone else was busy doing something else, and keep me company. He would help with the dishes without being asked, or volunteer for small chores, and tell me about school that day (Cubby liked to talk), and just altogether be a joy to have around.

One of those nights he was too preoccupied to be of much help. He came out to the kitchen, sat down on the tall stool (around the edge of which Annie had painted all their birthdays), and thought for a while. Then he made up his mind.

"Aunt Jane, I had this dream. Can I tell you about my dream?"

I allowed as how I'd listen to the dream.

"Well, there was this boy, a little boy — well, I don't know how old he was, exactly — but this boy got lost. Well, it was O.K. for a while, but then he began to get scared because he *really* wanted to get home, but nothing looked right, and he didn't know which direction to go in, and the farther he went, the more things looked different and not right, and then he *really* got scared because it started to get dark, and he didn't know *where* to go."

Cubby's brow was puckered with the effort to remember all the details of his nightmare.

"So he was in this dark old alley that he never was in before, and then it was getting cold, too, and he looked around and all he could see to hide in was this old messy dirty ucky old garbage can, and it was filled with smelly old garbage, but he didn't know where else to go, so he got in the garbage can with all the garbage, and then he was *really* scared, and he didn't know *what* to do, and it smelled awful, and he was all cold, and so he started to cry. And then..."

He paused and gave a sigh of relief, as if reliving the dream moment at that moment.

"...And then someone lifted up the top of the garbage can and reached down and lifted him out, and...well, I felt better right away and guess what, Aunt Jane, the lady who reached in the garbage can and picked me out was *you!*"

He finished this classic dream about abandonment and discovery, death and rebirth, in a rush of words to get to the marvelous, surprise happy ending. He wasn't aware that he had switched to the first person in midsentence. I stared at him in wonder at the superbly crafted gift his innocent psyche had given him, and on his face was the same expression of triumphant delight I had seen there when he caught his first fish. Tears were welling up and threatening to undo me. Again. That was happening altogether too often those days. It was one of

those rare magic moments of complete understanding between two people, never mind the
difference in age. I knew that Cubby's dream
was also a gift to me, his way of saying, "Take
me, I'm yours."

A gift like this needed an acceptance and a
thank-you. So I told him that actually I had
spent hours that very afternoon wandering
around in those backyards and alleys, in the
barn and in the attic, looking for something I
had lost, but I didn't know exactly what I was
looking for. And then I had a sudden hunch
that if I looked in that beat-up old garbage can,
I might find it. I might even find something
much better than whatever it was I thought I
was looking for. And so I went over to the garbage can and lifted the lid, and...guess what
it was? It was *you!*

I might have made up the particulars, but
the metaphor wasn't far off. I had had a dream
too, hadn't I? Though I didn't tell him mine
until much later.

The two of us, the thirty-six-year-old woman
and the nine-year-old boy, stood there beaming
at each other, as if we were sixteenth-century
explorers having found the way to the Spice
Islands, and then had some ice cream, just the
two of us. Later on, when Cubby was all grown
up and had majored in psychology and under-

stood about dreams, we talked about that numinous moment of mutual discovery, and what it had meant to each of us. For me, it was the first major emotional break-through in my new role as mother of seven. I had been accepted. It gave me hope for the future.

For Cubby, it was saying he had found his way home.

Thus Cubby freed himself from the bonds of grief much faster than his brothers and could go about normal development faster than they. He became an adult sooner than anyone, possibly including both Carl and me. While Ned and his buddy, Ken, were out laying waste the neighborhood, and John and his cohorts dominated the playing fields, Cubby got down to business. He had two good friends, Fred and Bobby, with similar mind-sets, and this trio soon cornered the village odd-job market. Odd Jobs, Inc., "We Do Anything Cheerfully," made itself ubiquitously useful. They were up at dawn mowing lawns, trimming hedges, weeding gardens, rebuilding stone walls, puttying windows, repairing broken anythings, painting houses, barns, and outhouses, babysitting, doing errands for old people, building reputations. Their business card could be found on every counter and bulletin board in town, and every household in the village, it seemed, found something for Odd Jobs to do. With seemingly unlimited energy, they covered the territory. They made a fortune (for nine-year-olds), working longer hours for less money than their more sophisticated, and lazier, older competitors, but they never felt exploited. Indeed they never were exploited. People liked having them around. Cubby quietly salted away his share of the profits in the big black piggy bank he had brought with him from New Jersey. Everyone knew where to go for a quick, friendly loan.

Cubby was almost too good to be true. "Have you taken your perfect pills today?" my friends would ask when they encountered him on his endless rounds, wagging their heads in wonder, signing him up for a week from Saturday. They were so delighted to be able to approve of something emanating from our house, after Ned's adventure with the homemade bomb, that they unanimously overdid it. But Cubby found time to have fun and get into minimal trouble, too, somewhat allaying the persistent fear that he might be perfect, though the suspicion never went away completely.

One aspect of the Cubby phenomenon was his luck. Who could explain it? When something got lost, Cubby found it. One day at the beach, a very big, very sandy beach, I lost a knitting needle. "Cubby," I said, joking, having given up looking, "will you please find my needle?" He went straight to it, yards away under the shifting sand and bronzing bodies.

No wonder he became everyone's favorite consultant. It began when he was nine and continued into adulthood. He would advise on how to invest money, what property to buy, how to build a house on it, who to marry, and what to have for dinner. Then he'd cook the dinner. No one ever figured out how he learned to cook, but he did. When Ned needed advice about buying property in Jamaica, it was Cubby who went and checked it out with him. When Ned later needed to settle down in the States, it was Cubby (with the invaluable help of his wife, Natalie) who found the right house for him. When Amy said, "Gee, I've always kind of liked Joe Squires," Cubby saw to it that his friend Joe came back from Alaska — yes — to go to her art show in New York that spring. The wedding took place two and a half years later, with Cubby as best man. When Nelly said she really admired Luke Porter's paintings, Cubby and Natalie arranged for the two to bump into each other easily — by inviting Luke, another friend of Cubby's, to live at their house, for one thing. That wedding took five years to materialize. It just went on and on like that.

When Cubby later confided to me that he

never in his wildest dreams could have hoped for better brothers-in-law than his two close friends Luke and Joe, it seemed to be in innocence of his own profound influence on the desired outcome. It was just Cubby's luck to get the best of all possible brothers-in-law. His luck spilled over, always, to include others. Everyone benefited. There's another word for this, of course; it's called empathy. But empathy with Cubby was so completely natural that it had the appearance of being his own good luck.

When Cubby was fourteen, he suddenly became harder to find on Saturday afternoons. Usually all I had to do to get a message to him (there were many) was call up a neighbor or go roaming around Main Street or Rendezvous Lane or, at the farthest, Salten Point Road, but suddenly he was nowhere to be found. People went around with puzzled looks on their faces, saying, "Where's Cubby?" Not even Fred or Bobby knew where he was. I figured his clientele must have expanded, maybe as far away as West Hyannisport, but I always forgot to ask when he came home.

One day he came through the back door with a particularly elastic gait, looking unusually pleased with himself, and coolly issued the blockbuster of the week: "I can fly!"

He hadn't been salting all his money away after all, but using a portion of it to buy flying lessons at Hyannis Aviation, a flight school at Barnstable Municipal Airport.

He progressed rapidly and as a result of this early training is now one of the relatively few airline pilots in the country who did not have to go into the Air Force to qualify for his job. When it came time for the Air Force to be an option, he already knew how to fly. He chose not to lend his skill to the military, since what the military was doing then was bombing North Vietnam. Cubby didn't think that was a reasonable way to spend his time. As for the draft, the luckiest lottery number an eligible young man could get was 365. Cubby got 352.

Cubby's ability to fly was one piece of his luck that overflowed particularly into my life. I was issued a parent's pass, one of the perks of a pilot's career, so I could fly almost anywhere I wanted for enormously discounted prices, and sometimes for nothing. It was like having a magic carpet. I needed one, considering how many people I had to keep track of, and how far flung they were at various times.

Cubby began his professional flying career with a small New England airline, but happened to leave just before that enterprise failed. He landed a job almost immediately with an unknown little upstart airline that has since become one of the fastest-growing airlines in the country. The deal included shares of stock, which naturally almost instantly doubled.

Somewhere along the line Cubby and two other pilots acquired their own plane. So then the magic carpet could be parked practically in the backyard. When Matt was on his way to college one September, everything he owned was stolen from his VW beetle in New York City. Cubby flew in some quickly assembled replacements the next day, landing his tiny single-engine Piper Cherokee 140, itself no larger than a VW with wings, at Philadelphia International Airport at rush hour.

I went along for the ride. Having long since learned not to worry when Cubby was in charge, I brought along my knitting. But then Cubby said, "Now, Aunt Jane, I want you to keep a sharp lookout to your right. If you see a plane coming, don't scream, just let me know." I put the knitting aside. This was a bit more than a spectator sport. The best part was climbing a huge black storm cloud just outside Philadelphia. I couldn't imagine how Cubby knew what was inside the cloud or on the other side of it or how tall it was, but he just kept climbing until he came out in the sunshine and down the other side, humming to himself the whole time.

When people asked me later if I was scared, the simple answer was "No. There was nothing to be scared of. I was with Cubby."

13

Paul

Rockabye baby, in the tree top,
When the wind blows,
the cradle will rock.
When the bough breaks,
the cradle will fall.
Down will come baby,
cradle and all.

Poor little Paulie-Boo was a mess. He was twenty-one months old when his parents died, and for most of those twenty-one months his mother had been terminally ill, his father frantic with worry over her and broke. Paul's care for the first crucial months of his life, then, had been in the hands of a sick mother, a harassed father, older brothers primarily interested in shaping their own identities, and a series of babysitters.

So what did he do when he arrived on Cape Cod with only part of this familial constellation intact, greeted by yet more strange faces and alien arms, an unfamiliar crib in a foreign room in some unknown place? He cried, naturally. He screamed. He shrieked. He sobbed. He banged his head and screamed again from the self-inflicted pain. After all, he had only recently arrived on the planet anyway, and life had been chaotic from the very beginning. How was he to know it wasn't to go on like this forever?

The most frightening and exhausting part of his infant grief was the head banging. I knew some babies did that, and even had a friend who was worried beyond reason about the gentle but insistent *thump-thump-thump* that her baby made on his crib mattress in the process of going to sleep. But Paul carried the syndrome several steps further.

The heating system of the old house consisted of hot water (sometimes) circulating in ugly cast-iron standing radiators that punctuated the wall space of every room in the house. Paul quickly discovered that if he toddled over to one of those radiators, reared his head back, and brought it crashing down on the hard metal edge, everyone came running. Of course it hurt. But it was worth it. That's how he kept someone in tow behind him every minute of the day, dedicated to keeping him from splitting his head open. He got away just often enough to have a permanent purple spot in the middle of his forehead, thus attracting even more sympathetic attention, but not often enough actually to kill himself. It got to be quite a game. After Paul emerged from that stage a survivor, I figured he had won.

It was a wonder that he didn't fracture his skull. I always believed that was what he was trying to do. On some deep level, his intent was to destroy himself. His sorrow was so profound, so unanswerable, that the only way he could express it was to hurt himself. Later on, I was to encounter research on depression in babies that seemed to confirm my early uneducated guess that even babies can be so depressed as to be suicidal. But Paul was saved by all those people chasing him and then loving him, and before long his universe straightened out, calmed down, became stable. He stopped trying to kill himself after about six weeks.

The most important stabilizer in Paul's new world was not his brothers, not me or Carl, not his cousins, but Rona, our maid. From the beginning, several of the relatives, especially the boys' grandmother, had insisted that we get some household help. Granny Willis even made me promise I would hire a maid as a precondition of the boys' coming to Barnstable, and sent money to pay for it. Up until then, my only help had been an occasional cleaning woman, and the latest one had promptly quit when she learned that four more children were moving in. But promising was one thing and actually finding the right person to help cope with this confusion was another. The pace of events was such that I couldn't even find the time to make the requisite phone calls.

A sympathetic neighbor, observing the jumble and muddle and welter in the big house on the corner, took on the impossible task of finding suitable help. One Monday morning on the dot of eight, amid the wild scramble of everyone's getting off to school, Rona showed up at the back door. She walked in, sized up the situation, and picked Paul out of his high chair moments before he would have flung himself from it in the direction of the nearest radiator. She took him upstairs to change his diapers without being asked, and when the two of them came back downstairs, Paul was rosy and clean and sweet smelling and in love. Carl and I had even had time for a cup of coffee — the height of our social life in those days. I was in awe of this miragelike personality who had instantaneously transformed my life. Rona asked where the flour and cinnamon were kept. She had her own priorities. I was more into eggs and orange juice and didn't have the slightest idea. She found them somehow, rolled up her sleeves, joggled Paul on one hip, and proceeded to make a one-handed coffee cake.

When the kids came home from school that day, the house smelled like a bakery, and word of Rona's unprecedented prowess with flour and cinnamon got around fast. The first two of Rona's famous "Specials" were consumed in a matter of minutes. In the meantime, Rona had soothed Paul into taking his first two-hour nap in weeks, had struggled with the mess of the house, and had started in on a mountain of mending. Rona, in short, was a marvel, just what the doctor ordered for everybody, but especially for Paulie-Boo. She made all the difference.

Paul grew and prospered. The purple spot in the middle of his forehead turned pink, turned a faint tan, went down, went away.

Just about the time it took for me to get used to having a new baby, Paul himself went away. In later years, those who heard the story of our expanded family always got confused about whether there were seven children or six. In the beginning there were seven, one for each day of the week.

But nine months after he arrived, Paul was gone. The circumstances of his leaving were so traumatic that I still can't talk about them without crying.

From the beginning, some of the boys' relatives were in favor of splitting them up. The very idea seemed an abomination, particularly to Ned, who, as new head of the family, received the letters from well-meaning people who wanted to take one or two of them, but especially the baby. Hadn't their mother, on her deathbed, instructed them to stick together?

The leading contender for getting Paul was a cousin of Ned Sr.'s, a lawyer who lived in Birmingham, Alabama, who had no children of his own. Cousin Louis and his wife had called Sara immediately when they heard of the tragedy and offered to take the baby. Other Birmingham relatives conferred with those in Indianapolis and New Jersey, and soon a considerable faction of relatives, all of the Willis branch of the family, were of the opinion that everybody would be better off if Paul went to Birmingham. Even my mother was enlisted by Granny Willis in Indianapolis to put the matter to Carl and me in the best possible light, i.e., that taking on all four was taking on too much, that "the baby would be a problem you shouldn't have to cope with," and that the big boys weren't really interested in Paul since there was such an age gap.

Sara, in particular, thought it was a wonderful idea to send Paul to Birmingham, a way, as she put it, of "spreading the wealth." She broached the suggestion on the very first day we met and was amazed when Carl and I rejected it out of hand. That was when I started to suspect that Sara viewed the present arrangement in Barnstable as strictly temporary, and that a more practical plan could be worked out once the dust settled.

She simply did not understand Carl's and my commitment to bringing the boys up together, as Carl had promised his sister he would do on the day she died. The very soul of practicality, Sara did not comprehend the power of that promise. She would never have made such an unrealistic pledge herself, and therefore it didn't exist for her. Nor did she comprehend the overwhelming importance to the boys of staying together, of maintaining their identity as a family, albeit absorbed into another family. The value to Ned and John and Cubby of being able to care for their little brother, to protect him, to make sure things went as well for him as could be expected, did not enter into the calculations of the "sensible" side of the family. Sara realized that it would be a mistake to break them up so soon, but she thought it was only a matter of time before the older boys got bored with their share of the responsibility and dumped it all on me, for whom it would be too much. Even in the midst of my irritation at their insensitivity, I knew that the practical people were trying to protect me. So I was grateful, angry, and upset, all at the same time.

For it was abundantly plain that the solidarity of the brothers was the single healthiest aspect of the new family montage. They might be adjusting in different ways, and maturing at uneven rates, but one thing above all else stood out about them, and that was their brotherhood. If that could be maintained, in Carl's and my opinion, they would emerge from the trauma strong and healthy. If not, they might collapse. Who knew, really? No one knew. It was a question of values. The values that were so clear to us were lost on Sara.

So the battle lines, though camouflaged by necessity and muted by grief, were drawn from the first. Carl and I seemed to be winning in the beginning. It seemed an inspired choice to everyone, what with children of the same ages, a big enough house, young enough parents, a father figure who was home all the time, plus our willingness. The other relatives were thankful, relieved, and admiring. Letters of sympathy, praise, congratulations, commiseration, and encouragement poured in. People sent gifts and money and offers of help. Visitors came clucking with concern and left beaming with approval. All seven kids were on their best behavior during those early months, everyone openheartedly determined to get along with everyone else. The house, with financial help from the relatives, got improvements and alterations to cope with the crowd, a process that was invigorating and exciting – every day something new. Christmas that year was an avalanche of love, of gifts and good feeling. It was an overreaction, of course, but it helped. Overreactions are not necessarily bad; you just pay for them later.

The opposition on the subject of keeping the boys together simply went underground. With the kids on their own turf, Carl and I won all the opening arguments. Since we were the ones taking the responsibility and doing the work, it seemed only fair that we should make the major decisions. Sara, having made her point, bided her time. The harsh realities of everyday life had not yet emerged. No one knew yet what the toll of the new togetherness would be.

The other relatives banded together and agreed to assist financially. That was a godsend, since we had no savings to speak of with which to meet the immediate needs of four more children. Ned and Annie had died intestate, which meant that it would be months, maybe years, before the legalities of straightening out the two estates would clear the courts. A prominent New Jersey law firm had been hired to file suit against the Jersey Central Railroad on the boys' behalf. But forty-nine other families were doing the same thing, and it was obvious that any settlement would take a while. There was a small life insurance claim to be filed, the house to be sold, and Social Security benefits to be claimed. The proceeds of all of these were predictably bound up in red tape, and would exist only sometime in the misty future, not then, when they were needed for food, clothing, books, and equipment, all of which were being used up daily in prodigious amounts. So we had to accept gratefully the financial help that was offered.

No one saw this financial arrangement as anything but temporary. It was the timing that mattered, and it was the timing that went askew. By April the money from the rest of the family started falling off. Apparently, the relatives assumed that the Social Security checks the boys began to get would cover expenses. By then the house in Rumson had been sold, which provided us with some capital. But the other crucial fact was that Carl's career had come to a grinding halt. This was altogether too sensitive an issue to discuss with virtual strangers, no matter how friendly they were because of mutual ties to the boys. So no one knew. At first.

For Carl and me, the tide was turning in a spooky way. It began to look as though our own children were the orphans and the Willis boys were the rich new kids who had come to town and gotten whatever they wanted. As one detail after another fell into place for Ned and John and Cubby and Paul, it seemed there was less and less for Matt and Amy and Nelly. And yet some kind of equity had to be maintained. We couldn't serve steak at one end of the table and macaroni at the other. Some of the family bene-factors were sensitive to this — making sure that whatever they made available to the Willises was also for the other children — but some weren't. And so Carl and I were forever off balance trying to make up the difference.

It wore on us. This was one of the harsh realities that Sara had known would rear its ugly head. Years later, when I consulted the old red and black bound ledger of those days in an effort to reconstruct our finances at the time and get a clearer understanding of what it was that made us think we could manage, I discovered some amazing figures, which I had mercifully not remembered longer than two minutes after recording them.

In 1957, our net income from writing, including a loan from Carl's agents, came to $3,909.86, and that was a vast improvement over 1956. The difference between that sum and what it took for us to live had come from a providential inheritance from Carl's father and from Carl's going to work for a public relations firm in Boston for seven months. By the time the fall of 1958 came around, that year's net income from writing had risen to $6,429.93 – slim pickings for a family of five, much less one of nine. Throughout that year and in 1959, we "dipped into" what we euphemistically referred to as "the savings." Wasn't that how all writers lived? It took me five years, what with the whirlwind of happenings, before I could look those figures in the eye, which was just as well, because if I had, I might have despaired, much less taken on more children. We didn't let ourselves think about the economics of what had to be done. We just did it. What we were really living on was hope. That was not so stupid because, as it turned out, the hope paid off in the long run. But not when we thought it would, or how we thought it would, not when we really needed it. And when the hope did come to fruition, our lives were so different as to be unrecognizable. From the perspective of 1958, and from any more objective point of view, hope was not going to be enough.

Sara, of course, had picked up on this simply by looking around. The old house was a shambles — comfortable, but a shambles. That was one of the reasons children loved it so much. No matter how much harm they did it, no amount of abuse seemed to change it much from the way it already was. It needed painting. There were no rugs on the floors or curtains on the windows. The furniture was hand-me-down mix and maybe match, and much of it was broken, scratched, cracked, or in various stages of disrepair. None of this bothered Carl and me very much because of the hope. I could always go shopping next month. But people dropping in couldn't help noticing.

Sara couldn't, although she was the soul of politeness and propriety. Her quiet observation that money was a bit scarce in this brave little household was added to the overall calculation of what would be best for everyone in the long run. She put it this way: Carl and I were financially naïve; we were going to have a rough time of it if we thought we could swing the extra responsibility. The relatives were only too happy to help for the time being, while it was a state of emergency. But they weren't prepared to make a long-term financial commitment, Sara said, especially if they were to have no effective say in the boys' futures. Even more especially if, deep in their hearts, they thought it was pure stubborn foolishness to try to keep all four together when a perfectly good home was being offered by a financially stable family who had no children of their own.

Paul would want for nothing. He would get his new mother's undivided attention. His affairs would be well attended to by a father who had full-time employment. All of this was said in the nicest possible way. But the implications were plain for all to see. In his present household, Paul would surely want for quite a lot. Kids get to a stage in life where they care about things like rugs and curtains. He certainly wouldn't get his present mother's undivided attention, even if such a thing existed. Judging from the turmoil of the place, who could guess how well his affairs would be tended to — or anyone else's, for that matter? If the relatives had seen the ledger, they would have gone into shock. Sara thought that eventually she might be able to do something to make things a little better, ease the strain somewhat. There was much to be said for her point of view, really.

Periodically, in one of her frequent phone calls to determine how things were, Sara would remind me that the offer from Birmingham still stood. The reminder was always politely noted and rejected, and Sara did not press the issue.

But it was like little drops of water eroding the landscape, turning a small fissure into a great canyon. Sara was right about how hard it would get. Early in the spring of 1959, Uncle Oscar, a trusted older friend, took Carl aside at a party and asked him whether he had taken a good look at his "bride" lately (that's what middle-aged wives were euphemistically called on Cape Cod in those days). The answer was no. Neither one of us had had time to look at the other recently.

"Well, I lost a wife myself once," Uncle Oscar said, choosing his words carefully. "Just be careful. You might be in more trouble than you think." Oscar had seen such a close resemblance between my worn-out look and that of his late wife during her terminal illness that he felt obliged to sound this solemn warning.

That was more than enough to reactivate Carl's intense but submerged guilt over what he had done to his neat little family. Never mind that he really *hadn't* done it; it had somehow been done. The guilt was lying there waiting to be picked up and put around someone's neck. So Carl picked it up and put it on. He looked at me across the crowded room, trying to have a carefree time and in the process getting sloshed and, seeing me through Oscar's eyes, had to admit that I did indeed look frazzled and faded. This was his *bride?* (Some expressions are pure poison.) He caught his own reflection in a mirror as he headed for the bar to get another drink, and a skeleton's head stared back at him. "You don't look so hot yourself, Sport," the apparition muttered as it passed.

What was to be done? We were both exhausted and simply didn't know what to do. Carl's writing was at a standstill, and it was getting harder and harder to maintain the hope that it would ever get better. By that spring of 1959, he had earned $300 in options for the year. We were living by selling stock that he had inherited from his mother many years before, our safety net. At that rate, the safety net would not hold for long. A settlement with the railroad was still a matter of speculation. The Social Security checks did not in fact make up the difference.

Carl did not tell me about his conversation with Uncle Oscar, thinking it would somehow make things worse. But he worried. He couldn't work for worrying. The slow flow of creative juice, just beginning to pick up since his sister's death, congealed.

Before Uncle Oscar's well-intentioned candor, we had both been thinking we were doing pretty well, considering. A crisis is a crisis is a crisis, and one must make allowances for it. Optimism kept rearing its silly head, no matter what. The boys themselves were getting along remarkably well, adjusting smoothly to their new home, cousins, school, the neighborhood, the community. The kids were having a good time together. Our own three children were holding their own, enjoying their roles as brother, sisters, cousins, and protectors. Carl and I were on the whole more pleased (consciously) with the way the experiment in living was working than we were upset (subconsciously) by its problems and inconveniences. We were proud of ourselves for pulling off "Mission Impossible" so skillfully. True, it was no bed of roses, but who had promised us a rose garden? We still had that fathomless reservoir of hope we had been drawing our energy from for so long. If only...if only Carl could get back to work. But meanwhile, what to do?

Then one day came what looked very much like a break; at least it was a chance for one of us to take a break. One of Carl's oldest and best friends had had a hip operation and had been invited to recuperate at the home of another mutual friend, a writer, in Florida. Jack, who was an editor, asked Carl to go with him, since he could not drive himself from New York to Sarasota and would welcome the companionship. Also, they could talk shop. Jack was aware of our situation and concerned with ways of getting Carl's career out of the doldrums. It did not take Carl and me long to decide that this was a golden opportunity for him to get away for a few days, have a breather, maybe acquire a new perspective on our predicament. It was out of the question for both of us to take a vacation at that point, and one was better than none. So, on Sunday, May 3, 1959, Carl took off for Florida, leaving me to deal with things alone for the first time.

There was a lot to do. John had just made the most elite of the four local Little League teams, Dumont's Pharmacy, and had to be transported to the field every day at five-thirty. Cubby was trying out for the farm team — at another field, of course. Matt was about to have his thirteenth birthday, and plans were under way for a giant cookout. Nelly was about to graduate from nursery school and needed a new dress. Amy was on the planning committee for the Brownies' Spring Event, so she had to learn how to make cookies over an open fire. Sandy had gotten into another dog fight and had to be taken to the vet's to have his ear sewed up. And the hot water heater burst its poor old seams and flooded the basement just when everyone needed a bath.

In short, it started off just like any other week for me.

The second evening, needing some quiet form of escape after delivering everyone to their various practices, appointments, and rehearsals, I conned Ned into taking care of Paul and slipped away to a friend's house for dinner. Just as we were sitting down, the phone rang. It was Sara calling for me. Ned had had the call forwarded. There was no escape, not even for a few hours.

Sara was all cheeriness and enthusiasm, as was her wont, inquiring about everyone and letting me know that things were great in New Jersey. Then I found out why.

"I have the most wonderful news!" she said enthusiastically. "Louis can come for the baby tomorrow!"

Louis was the Birmingham cousin, but I had forgotten his name. I had no idea what Sara was talking about.

"Huh?"

"Louis will be there tomorrow for the baby,"

she repeated. "Isn't that the luckiest thing?"

Then I remembered who Louis was, but incomprehension set in again. I could not understand what was being said to me.

"What are you *talking* about? What do you *mean*, Louis will be here for the baby?"

"You mean you didn't know? But Carl said it was all right. Carl said, 'Fine, go ahead.' He called on his way through New York. He said Louis could have the baby. So I went ahead and called Louis. He will be there tomorrow."

For the second time in my life, a telephone call from New Jersey had thrust me into a full-blown nightmare. I couldn't believe it. Carl would not have made that decision without my agreement, much less without even telling me. Sara had to be lying. But Sara didn't lie. Sara was too noble to lie, always thinking of everyone's good. But this couldn't possibly be true. What had happened?

If I had to choose between two people I thought I could trust, I would choose my husband. I told Sara as calmly as I could that no such decision had been made, that she must have misunderstood, that what she was suggesting was unthinkable. Then I realized I was shouting into the telephone. I hung up and fell apart.

All the negative emotions that I had carefully

repressed during the past nine months of fervent coping now emerged in full fury. I had not let myself be angry when anger was called for, had not let myself feel vulnerable or ambivalent, would not admit any feelings of thwarted self-interest, would not, would not, would not be weak or self-pitying, all in the service of making the family work. I had abandoned all of my personal goals, all of them (including the soundness of my marriage, it sometimes seemed), in order to do it. And now my supreme effort was being sabotaged. The threat of losing Paul, now that I had had him for nine months, long enough to have actually given birth to him, ripped through the veil of numbness behind which I had sought to protect myself. I realized with profound shock that I had never been so angry in my life. I was not very good at dealing with my own anger, never had been. Now even I could see it, plain as electric sparks flying from steel wheels grinding on steel rails in the night, trying to stop, trying to stop.

The dinner party was over. It turned instantly into a crisis intervention session. Everyone had a different idea about what to do.

First, find Carl. Find out what had happened. Had he called Sara? If he had, what had he said?

Second, call Sara back. Tell her to stop Louis from coming. Whatever Carl had said, it was a mistake.

We started dialing numbers of places in New York, New Jersey, Maryland, and Washington where we thought Carl might be. Either he had just left, or hadn't arrived yet, or was not expected. The most informed guess was that he was somewhere near Baltimore by then. We left messages everywhere.

I had a stiff drink of Scotch, pulled myself together, and called Sara back. I apologized for flying off the handle and tried again to get through to her the enormity of what she had done. As patiently as I could, I explained where Carl and I stood on the issue and admitted that things had been hard, but not *that* hard. We might have had a small suspicion that we would have to re-evaluate our position sometime, but we hadn't done it yet. No matter how it might all turn out in the future, it was out of the question for Louis to come get the baby tomorrow.

I felt myself losing control again. The brief spurt of false courage the Scotch had afforded me was dissipating. I tried to explain to Sara, who should have known, what this would mean to the other boys: another staggering overnight bolt from the blue. It would be as hard for them, in its way, as losing their parents —

harder, in that it would be a blow deliberately dealt them by loved ones whom they had come to trust, instead of being an inexplicable act of God. But this blow could be avoided. I told Sara she had to call Louis and tell him not to come. Now.

"I don't even know him. He can't have the baby tomorrow."

"But I know him. You don't trust me."

She kept repeating "you don't trust me" in a grieved tone.

I was getting nowhere. Sara's stubborn inability to understand anything but her own point of view was astonishing. I gave up and asked to speak to Calvin.

Calvin was more sympathetic. He seemed to have an inkling that strong feelings were involved here, that this proposed move was more significant than a simple redistribution of family goods — at the mover's convenience. He agreed to call Louis in Birmingham and explain to him that there had been a misunderstanding and that Louis should call off his trip. I wept with relief.

But fifteen minutes later, Calvin called back. He had tried to reach Louis, but Louis had already left. Apparently, he had cleared his calendar for the next two days, packed a bag, and boarded a plane for Boston within an hour after hearing from Sara that he could have the baby.

A double search was now under way. I and my friends, with the emergency help of AT&T, located dimly remembered names and lost telephone numbers and left a trail of messages for Carl down the eastern seaboard. Sara said she would try to locate Louis in Boston. I didn't believe her. If I had learned anything in the last two frantic hours, it was to be more careful with my trust. I was convinced that as far as Sara was concerned, the transfer of the baby was a *fait accompli*. It was, after all, in everyone's best interest. Besides, she liked to win.

The situation was not only intolerable; it was bizarre. What did this man who had never had children, who was coming without his wife, know about caring for, feeding, even *holding* a two-and-a-half-year-old? My thoughts turned to the boys. If this stranger was really going to show up in the morning, they had to be prepared. Sara had been careful to specify the exact details of Louis's arrival: West Barnstable train station, 10:15 A.M., the express from Boston. I would, of course, be at the station to meet him.

I was feeling very shaky when I left my friends' house that evening. I ate little and left early, knowing that I needed time alone with each boy to explain what was happening to them as best I could. They would hate me for letting it happen. I felt utterly betrayed, in an intolerable position. The worst of it was wondering what Carl had said to Sara to make her feel justified in going to such lengths. I dismissed the awful thought, almost before I had it, that he had capitulated without telling me. What on earth had he said? How could he leave me in a mess like this?

Ned had fallen asleep over his homework. I roused him and told him the whole story. I needed an ally. He was marvelously responsive, appropriately outraged, sympathetic to my plight, intuitively responsible about how to put it to the two younger boys, protective of the baby, and accepting of the surmise that Sara had wildly misinterpreted whatever Carl had said. We decided not to wake the other boys but to wait until morning and tell them separately. Ned would tell John and I would tell Cubby. It seemed important that each be told on a level that matched his own understanding of the whole situation, and that each have an opportunity to say how he felt and to ask whatever questions he needed to, in private. Both Ned and I wanted to avoid a scene that in any way resembled the last bolt from the blue.

The next day was Tuesday, a school day. I

was up early, groggy from a wakeful night of rehashing the conversations of the night before, rehearsing the more difficult ones ahead. I had finally taken a tranquilizer to get a few hours' sleep. When Cubby appeared for breakfast, I greeted him with an invitation to take a walk down the lane.

He looked puzzled, as well he might have, since early-morning-before-school walks were not a regular feature of our life. It was a lovely spring morning, which helped, but not much.

Cubby received the news with bewilderment and tears. He simply couldn't understand it. He didn't know who Uncle Louis was, why anyone would send Paul to live anywhere else, why Aunt Sara would think it was a good idea, how Uncle Carl could have said it was O.K., or how come I was allowing it to get this far. It was almost impossible for me to explain any of these enigmas to Cubby, whose adoration of Aunt Sara enormously complicated the task. I felt I couldn't really tell him the whole story, or what I thought was the whole story at the time, because I didn't want to undermine his feelings for the aunt who was, after all, one of the most important people in his life. Also, he had no way of comprehending, at age nine, the financial ramifications. It had been helpful for me to be able to be candid with Ned, who was old enough to understand about money. Even beginning to discuss the possibility of giving Paul away in that context would have made him feel even more insecure, would have turned Carl and me into Scrooges in his eyes. I couldn't take that risk. With tears in his eyes, Cubby ended the conversation by saying, "I know you'll do what's best, Aunt Jane. But I don't want Paul to go, and I'm not going to school today, and I don't care whether this guy comes from Alabama or not, but he can't have my brother." Cubby broke away from me and raced back to the house and upstairs to be with Ned and John.

Ned's talk with John, which had been taking place simultaneously in John's room, ended much the same way, with the difference that John was more angry than bewildered, partly because Ned did tell him about Aunt Sara's role in more detail. John bellowed and cried and smote the wall with his fist, causing it to rain plaster downstairs. He was furious with me, assuming that this would not be happening unless I had somehow permitted it to happen. He also announced that he was not going to school that day. He was not going to stand by and let someone he had never heard of kidnap his baby brother.

With the introduction of the word "kidnap"

came the full realization of the ugliness of this thing. It was nothing less than a genteel kidnapping, sanitized by having been arranged by relatives. The ransom was their pride, their autonomy as a family unit. That autonomy was so hard won, so vulnerable a thing...and Sara had taken a hacksaw to it. She had waited until the man of the family was out of town and had told a stranger he could have their baby. Undoubtedly, the reason for Louis's hurried departure was to get the operation accomplished fast, before Carl got home. Sara was counting on my having no backbone. She had counted wrong.

By the time the family gathered in the kitchen, emotions were more stirred up than they had ever been in the past nine months. The imminent kidnapping brought back afresh the trauma of September, gave it an outlet and a focus. Everyone felt the same grief and rage. If the original tragedy had caught them unprepared and impotent, this one wouldn't. Something could be done about this one: namely, they wouldn't let this stranger from Alabama have the baby. By this time, Matt and Amy had been informed, and they joined the chorus. Paul was their baby brother, too; if Ned and John and Cubby weren't going to school, neither were they. Who does this Louis think he is, anyway? Outrage. Tears.

It was nine-thirty. I had to leave in twenty minutes to meet the train with the villain on it. The phone rang.

It was Carl. AT&T had finally found him. He had arrived at Sarasota about an hour earlier, having driven all night. His immediate plan was to take a nap and then get out in the sun, go fishing, talk with the other writers there.

I told him what was happening at my end. He exploded with frustrated rage. I had never heard him so angry. Witnesses at his end said they had never seen anything like it. The substance of what he had to say was that he had not given Sara permission to do this. He had called her and they had discussed the situation. For the first time, he had acknowledged to Sara the extent of the problem, but he had not agreed to let the baby go. Sara had absolutely misunderstood and overstepped herself. Both. Under no circumstances was I to let the baby go.

"I'll be home as fast as I can," he said.

End of vacation.

The call was just what I needed to muster the strength to meet the train. The *Gaslight* feeling of having been tricked into this intolerable spot evaporated. At least I knew that Carl had not done this to me. My faith in him was justified.

It made me even more infuriated with Sara that my trust in Carl had been so cruelly put to the test.

Shaking, I left for the train station, rehearsing lines on the way. I went alone, needing the time to figure out what to say. How on earth was I going to explain this disaccord to Louis? Would he understand? What was Louis like? For the first time, I contemplated the reality of the new person on my horizon. How was I to handle him? All Sara had said about him, really, was "Trust me."

I had to wait only three minutes before the train pulled into the rattletrap West Barnstable station. One person got off. He was a slightly built, dark-haired, good-looking man, in his early forties I guessed, conservatively dressed in lawyerly gray flannels, with a slightly receding hairline and an anxious look on his face. We smiled tentatively at each other, and we knew that was our introduction. With a quick flick of his wrist, he glanced at his watch.

"Jane?"

"Louis?"

"Who else."

"Well, hello."

"There's a train back to Boston in an hour and a half. If you can have the baby ready by then, I can catch it."

Staggering, I drew a long breath.

"I'm sorry, that won't be possible. Louis, I have to say it fast. There has been a mistake. Sara got it wrong. I tried to stop you. You had left. It's not all right. Carl did not tell Sara to tell you to come. He's not here. He's in Florida. But he just called. He's coming right back. He told me not to let the baby go. I wasn't going to anyhow. I will try to explain."

I stopped for a breath. Louis was listening to me patiently, standing there on the weather-beaten old platform, his brow creased. The train had left, panting on to Hyannis. The place was deserted except for the two of us.

"You have no idea what this means to the other boys. You have no idea about any of this, period, or you wouldn't be here. I don't know what's going to happen in the long run. I only know for sure that you can't have the baby now. If you have to catch the next train back, it will be without the baby."

Louis did not remonstrate. He seemed to be a man who listened well, whose mode was to try to understand what was being said of him. I liked him. I felt a rush of relief at his receptiveness, his obvious decency. In the stress of the moment we had become instant friends. The words flew out of me too fast for anyone but a talented listener to absorb.

Louis accepted immediately the hard truth that he was not going to catch the next train back to Boston. He acknowledged that he needed time to get to know Paul and the other boys, and that he needed to know the family before it would be at all reasonable to expect to take the baby. He did not even seem to be surprised by any of this, but rather challenged by a more complex state of affairs than he had been given to understand existed. He simply said that he needed to make a phone call to cancel his appointments for the next few days.

Louis was willing to wait.

My recapitulation of the entire situation, beginning with the early days in New Jersey, extending through how everyone felt that May morning on Cape Cod, and including the strong feelings of all the children, had to be compressed into the fifteen minutes it took to drive home from the station. When we pulled into the driveway, I felt I had done the best I could to equip him with the information he needed to deal with the ticklish confrontation ahead.

As we walked through the back door into the kitchen, we were greeted with total, silent hostility. The kids, whether by accident or design I never found out, had arranged themselves in a semicircle more or less by size, starting with Ned, at six feet three inches, and ending with

Paul, barely two feet off the floor. Ned had on his most defiant expression. In between were ranged John, Matt, Cubby, Amy, Nelly, and two of my friends who had come to help me through the ordeal. On everyone's faces were expressions of anger, hurt, apprehension, and dislike. It looked as if Cubby and Amy had been crying. I broke the silence with perhaps the most unnecessary introduction in the history of the family.

"Well, everybody, this is Louis."

No one said a word. Then something happened that turned the tide and saved the day, and that no one could believe at the time, and that no one could ever forget.

Little Paul looked around and must have noticed that in this place of usually cheery greetings and much movement, no one had moved and no one had spoken. It must have seemed strange to him and in need of fixing. Who can know what went through his thirty-month-old consciousness? He broke away from the frozen ring of resistance and ran across the room, a streak of yellow in his fuzzy Dr. Dentons, and flung his arms around Louis's knees, almost knocking him down with the force of the unexpected embrace.

Be as little children, you dolts. With Paul as role model and pacesetter, everyone was suddenly galvanized into speech and action. The ice was broken, the lynch-mob mood lifted, in an instantaneous recognition that the only way to be was decent. Meanwhile, Louis was reinforcing this by being utterly gracious and understanding of the difficulty they were all having with the fact of him.

He could not take his eyes off Paul, who was larger than life. He could not believe the reality of his adorable toddler, of whom he felt destined to be father. He moved into the role so naturally that no one could say when, exactly, the decision was made.

As that day and the next one passed, it became clear, although no one articulated it until after Carl came home, that this was going to work out somehow. Louis made a point of getting acquainted with them all, separately and as a group. That night at dinner, he sat at the head of the table, in Carl's empty place, and carved a roast that seemed to have appeared from nowhere. The conversation grew steadily less and less strained, with more and more delicate areas capable of being discussed. Louis conceded his inexperience with children so openly, with so much quiet competence underlying the concession, that I believed he *was* capable of managing Paul.

By the time Carl arrived, by bus, plane, and

train, at 10:45 the following night, Louis had won their hearts. There was a great deal to be gone over nevertheless: information exchanged, details worked out, assurances made. Carl and Louis needed to build a rapport, which they did. The three of us stayed up almost all night getting to know one another, and ultimately making the momentous decision to transfer Paul's young life into Louis's care. It had become agonizingly plain that Paul would in the long run be better off, just as Sara had said he would be. So much had been dragged out in the open that couldn't be stuffed back into subconsciousness again.

Even the children, though they hated the decision, couldn't argue anymore. Louis had proved to their complete satisfaction that he cared enough to be Paul's father, and that his wife, Cathy, who had frequently been consulted by telephone, was equally caring. Crucial to the final understanding was Carl's and my insistence, and Louis's and Cathy's agreement, that Paul would be brought up knowing the truth, that his parents by birth had died, that he had three brothers and close relatives in Massachusetts. Above all, he was to be not only permitted but encouraged to stay in touch with them.

All of this has come to pass.

But the decision to give up Paul was perhaps the most difficult I've ever had to make. Light-years more difficult than the one to take the children in the first place.

Years later, a psychotherapist asked me why. After all, the doctor said, you're not the one who made the promise to keep all the children together. Why did you so internalize this promise that *someone else had made* without assessing the probable consequences, or without even questioning your own ability to deal with them? Where were your own decision-making powers and your own ability to analyze the realities of your own situation? Good questions, ones that did not get asked, much less answered, at the time. All I could say, lamely, when the questions finally were asked, was that I wasn't into reality in those days.

I had been seduced by the conditions of my marriage into one romantic illusion after another. Our days were concoctions of heroic illusions, and I had believed that the Iceman would never come. Sara had taken on the role of the Iceman who did come, and what I hated her for was not so much that she had Paul taken away, but that she had so rudely torn a hole in the veil of precious illusion that had kept us safe.

Had I been able to ask those hard questions at the appropriate time, the marriage might not have dissolved twelve years later. But then again, had I ever been able to ask a hard question, the marriage might never have happened in the first place. Thus did the Paul crisis shed light both ahead on a future disaster and back on past mistakes. The veil had been rent.

But Carl and I and Louis and Ned and all the others thought we had dealt with the emergency reasonably well. It was arranged that Ned and I would drive Louis and Paul to a relative's house near Boston and there part, while the other kids went back to school and Carl went back to work.

It was Ned who helped me pack Paul's things, his little shirts and sleepers and sheets and toys, and as we did it, I felt as if I were packing away everyone's babyhood, including my own, and saying goodbye to it. Carl was already back in his study at his typewriter, almost as if this was something that was not happening. He got more and more like that as time went by. He had to. His defense against painful events was to pretend they didn't exist. I had to do the packing, then and later.

Babyhood does not end so suddenly in most households, except when the baby dies. It was like a death in the family, yet another death. But it was a necessary loss.

There were aspects of Paul's departure that were never clear, and that remain shrouded in mystery to this day. The problem was that everyone involved remembered the events and the circumstances leading up to it differently.

As I prepared to write it all down, I interviewed them all, matching memories and searching for the truth of the matter. I traveled to Summit, New Jersey, for a long delayed reunion with Sara and Calvin, to clarify what their perspective had been. I was amazed to hear their version of the story.

"Don't you remember when you came to see us in the motel on Route 132 when Carl was away and you cried and cried?" Sara asked me. "Don't you remember telling us you were at your wits' end? You said Carl didn't want *any* of the children! You said he wanted to give away all seven of them! We were shocked. We went right back and called Louis, and he asked how many he could have. He came right up for Paul."

No, I said. I didn't remember saying any such thing. I didn't remember Carl saying any such thing. I was so stunned by this interpretation that I dug up my old 1959 calendar book to find out when Sara and Calvin had been there. There it was. They had visited the Cape on April 3 and 4, 1959, and had stayed at the Top o' the Morn Motor Lodge on Route 132. But Carl had not been away at that time. And Louis had not come for the baby until May 5. That part I did remember, vividly, since it was one of the worst days of my life.

Sara and Calvin were surprised to learn that a month had gone by between when they heard how bad things were and when Louis had been notified. They didn't recall Carl calling them on May 4. I was surprised to learn what I had said when I visited the motel (I did remember going there).

Yet no one was consciously trying to deceive anyone else. Each of us remembered the same thing differently because self-interest was at stake all along the line.

There were more surprises.

"Don't you remember," asked Sara, "the time Paul was lost? No one could find him anywhere, and we thought he might have fallen in the pond. We were all down there looking in the bushes, frantic. And then it turned out Nelly had taken him and put him in some neighbor's house."

No, I said. I didn't recall that at all. I thought Nelly had probably just taken Paul with her to a friend's house to play. But it must have looked different to the relatives from New Jersey, who thought Paul belonged somewhere else anyway.

More like a murder attempt.

"And don't you remember," asked Sara, "the time Nelly drank something corrosive, like Clorox or Sani-Flush, or something awful like that, and you had to rush her to the hospital to have her stomach flushed out? The doctor told you you had to pay more attention to her — she's trying to get attention?"

I had no memory of that at all.

"It's hardly the kind of thing a mother would forget," said Sara.

"True," I said. I thought Sara might have gotten the story about Matt eating the mushrooms growing outside the back door when he was a baby and having to have his stomach pumped (only to discover the mushrooms were "wholesome and delicious") mixed up with something Nelly did. Or with the time Ned threw ammonia in John's face.

Nelly, asked to remember twenty-seven years later, didn't recall it either. But something severely untoward must have happened in that bemused household to cause Sara and Calvin to put such a construction on it: Suicidal Four-year-old Attempts to Murder Baby!

What well-organized woman wouldn't want to step in and save them both?

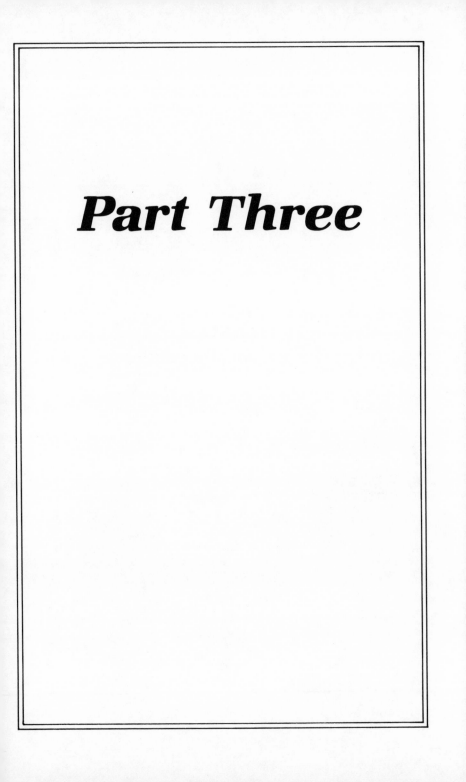

Part Three

14

On Memory

When to the sessions of sweet silent
    thought
I summon up remembrance of
    things past,
I sigh the lack of many a thing I
    sought,
And with old woes new wail my dear
    times' waste.
                  William Shakespeare
                  Sonnet 30

The human brain is a strange and wonderful and amazing natural event, so to speak, " 'an enchanted loom' weaving ever-changing yet always meaningful patterns — weaving, in effect, patterns of meaning."* Indeed, the very words describing its parts — cerebrum, corpus cal-

*Oliver Sacks, *The Man Who Mistook His Wife for a Hat*, quoting C. S. Sherrington, *Man on His Nature.*

209

losum, cortex, cerebellum, medulla oblongata — sound like the movements of a symphony, and they do work together to produce for each of us totally individual harmonies that take a lifetime to play out. And within that mass of nervous tissue, that maze of neurons and synapses, those three pounds of stuff (2 percent of total body weight) that in its infinite complexity is what most distinguishes us from our fellow creatures, perhaps the most mysterious area is where memory resides. Memory, dreams, imagination: sometimes they seem interchangeable.

Each person's memory is unarguably unique to him or her. And as I discovered in digging for the truth, particularly in writing the chapter on Paul, each person's memory seems to serve that person's ego. Just as any marriage is not just one marriage, but at least four — his, hers, theirs, and the one they show to the world — so any one event will carry with it as many different interpretations as there are people who experienced it. So what is the truth about any given event? God knows. Perhaps that is one of the prime motivations for believing in God: the overwhelming need that human beings have for thinking that Someone really knows what's going on.

But this variety of interpretation is just one of the problems. Memories will trick even the most adroit rememberers. One memory will stand out in crystal clarity, as real as if the thing remembered happened only yesterday; another will dig itself into the sands of time and never come back up. It doesn't even have that much to do with whether the memories are good or bad ones. It would be lovely if we could bury only the bad ones and cherish the good ones in living color forever. But that's not the way it works. Some people seem to remember predominantly the good times, others mainly the bad. Which ones you keep forever seems to have more to do with whether you're basically an optimist or a pessimist and less to do with the quality of the memories themselves, or with which ones best serve your self-image, regardless of the truth.

As I discovered when it came time to write about my children, this is only the beginning of the problems when you get involved with your memory. I discovered to my dismay (because I thought it was going to be easy) that my memories of my own children, as children, were not nearly as clear as my memories of the children I acquired "by accident."

It was as if each of the Willis boys, at the ages of fourteen, eleven, nine, and one and a half, had been brightly illuminated by a brilliant streak of lightning generated by the power of the tragedy – especially at those moments of insight, of emotional breakthrough, when I knew that they had taken me and their new family into their hearts.

But my own children I had known intimately since I had first felt them move within me. There was no special streak of lightning for them, no sudden revelation unforgettable in its intensity. Luminosity, yes; that wonderful love at first sight, and then a slow-growing, ever-growing, steady glow of understanding and delight and pride as they changed from infants to children, to adolescents, to young adults. But no electrifying flashes.

And to make matters even more perplexing, as I tried to capture in words the essence of each, I realized that my own ego was inextricably bound up with them. Wasn't it just a touch too self-congratulatory to say what I really felt: that they were surely three of the most extraordinary, marvelously complicated, lovable human beings ever to have come to earth? How hard can you pat yourself on the back without falling down? Because, as every mother knows, a compliment to your child is a compliment to you. And what about their faults, their flaws, which in my more lucid moments I realized existed? How to handle the guilt?

By knowing better than to take it on, I said to myself. By knowing how thoroughly they are their own selves, how much, much, more themselves than a reflection of me or of their father.

But how to be objective, immersed as I was in so many subjective thoughts and feelings, in the love and the responsibility? Probably there is no way. Nevertheless, it had become necessary to try, to try to put into words who these remarkable people were. In the process, I discovered why so few parents become their children's biographers.

15

Matt

The message part of grace was something I was never quite at home with. I was perfectly comfortable when it seemed like just a simple greeting.

"Hi, Matt."

"Hi, God."

And that would be that. It wasn't a one-sided affair. I could start it.

"Hi, God."

And usually he'd come back, "Hi, Matt."

Not always, but there were probably plenty of times He said "Hi" and I missed it.

From Matt's book

When the dust cleared, years later, it turned out that the hardest hit of all the children was Matt. At twelve, Matt had become adjusted to being the oldest child and only son in a manageable if slightly eccentric little family of five that overnight blew its boundaries.

Matt was a serious, quiet boy, a loner, brilliant at math and already occasionally able to beat his father at chess. Only marginally athletic (because his natural athletic ability was never encouraged by either parent), he prided himself on his ability to defend himself in fistfights. Matt felt called upon to defend himself often when he was very young. He acted out the role of "new kid in town" for four years, two years longer than was necessitated by the facts. In truth, he had traveled more by the time he went to nursery school than generations of Cape Codders had, ever.

He was born in Chicago, moved to a suburb of Schenectady when he was less than a year old, thence to Provincetown, Massachusetts, when he was four, and on to Osterville at five. In the first grade in Osterville he was really no newer than anyone else, having attended the School for Tiny Tots the year before along with all the old-timers. But he still felt like the new kid in town. The title was again legitimately his when he entered the third grade at the Barnstable Elementary School, all of seven miles away, two years later. This special agony should have been over by the time he began the fourth grade, but it continued.

Part of the reason for his sense of isolation must have been his identification with his father, who, being a writer, felt like an outsider wherever he was. Matt became conscious early on that his parents were different from his schoolmates' parents – Democrats in a sea of Republicans, liberals in an overwhelmingly conservative area (except for one little patch of Hyannisport), the last people in the village to acquire a television set, and then only to watch the McCarthy hearings. They didn't go to church. They didn't have a boat. His father stayed home all day and wrote while the other kids' fathers went off somewhere every day and *worked.*

So Matt felt different and alone. He reacted to every schoolyard taunt and took on all comers. It was a vicious circle. The more he felt called upon to defend himself, the better he got at it. The more he was the Kid to Fight, the better he got at it. The greater a challenge it was to beat him up, the better he got at it. And on and on. He never came home with his tail between his legs or asked his father or me to bail him out. But what he really wanted to do was to go fishing by himself or with a friend who wouldn't always be punching him.

My first real heartbreak in connection with

Matt was when, at the age of ten, he solemnly told me at bedtime one night that he'd really just as soon be dead. His brown eyes were swimming with tears. What was a mother to do? I promised him that it would change. I couldn't tell him in what way it would change, only that it would. It was a real promise, as far as I could go by way of promising then, and it seemed to help.

So Matt's original world view placed him definitively: he was the oldest, the biggest, the strongest, the toughest, and the smartest of the siblings. Since he was the only boy, it was a lonely role. He prized his solitude. He told himself it was up to him to figure things out, make his own way, and then help out as best he could those smaller, weaker, dumber ones who came after him. He was confident of his ability to live up to this heroically strict self-definition. He was an utterly competent oldest child and big brother, even if he had his weak moments.

And then.

And then, knocking his world to smithereens, shattering his self-image, turning everything topsy-turvy in a whirlwind of unpredictable dimensions, along came not one, not two, not three, but four young males usurping his position in innumerable complicated ways. To add insult to injury, he was apparently expected to regard them as brothers, a relationship with which he had had no experience. Two of these teeming intruders turned out to be bigger and stronger than he. The other two just confused the issue.

None of the subterranean emotions connected with Matt's displacement as oldest child and only son and strongest sibling were immediately manifest. How could they be when the whole family was confronted with the spectacle of four orphaned little boys? Matt's heart went out to his cousins along with all the other hearts in the neighborhood. Ned and John and Cubby were terrific kids. Everybody liked them. Who wouldn't? Who wouldn't be proud to have them become part of his family? Who wouldn't be happy to move out of his room so that poor John could have a room of his own? Who wouldn't try to become less belligerent and more popular at school so that his own unpopularity wouldn't carry over to the orphans? Who wouldn't suddenly become a regular hail-fellow-well-met so as not to prejudice the entire school against the new "new boys"?

Certainly not Matt. Matt didn't want his odd-ball status to contaminate his cousins, so he quickly, quietly, and efficiently moved out of it. Suddenly he was sort of popular.

The combative streak in Matt went underground, and he was all hospitality, generosity, warmth, and pride. No one needed his protection anymore. Instead of being the Lone Ranger hero, he was only one of a phalanx of stalwarts at the beck and call of two little girls who had been transformed into princesses at the ball.

As for the family honor, it was taking care of itself, thank you. Nothing more thrilling had happened in the village since Henry Crocker put gunpowder in the top of his woodpile to discourage the thief who had been stealing his wood regularly. The deviant family whose father stayed home and wrote all day had proved itself by taking in the four orphans. Never mind that they belonged to no church. Suddenly people thronged through the back door bearing lemon meringue pies, and it seemed to Matt that his parents had been transformed by the tragedy from being outsiders to being quintessential insiders.

An astute child psychologist might have guessed that Matt preferred the bittersweet old days to these heady new ones, and might even have suggested remedial measures. But there was no child psychologist on the premises, or anywhere around, although the need for one shrieked from the groaning floorboards. The assumption was, of course, that everyone would have preferred the good old days, when no one had died and when everyone's mothers and fathers were in their proper places. The assumption was that the emotional burden of the deaths simply had to be sustained, shared and shared alike by everyone involved. The burden was indeed shared, but far from equally. Matt took more than his share.

I overheard a conversation between Matt and John one night when the boys, who at that point shared a room, had gone to bed. Matt was asking awkward, tentative questions about what it was like to be John, clearly trying to get a better measure of his cousin-brother-orphan-hero-superrival. John was just as clearly trying to get out of the conversation, brushing off Matt's questions with noncommittal though not hostile comments. John was still in his distant stage and desperately hanging on to it and was not about to allow any intimacy with anyone in this so-called new family, much less with this embarrassingly smaller cousin who couldn't even hit or catch a ball right. John associated only with kids who could play ball. It was painful to hear, and I wished I hadn't lingered outside the door, except that I needed to know what it hurt to hear.

It was around then that the extent of Matt's nearsightedness surfaced. It took John to discover one day that the reason Matt couldn't hit a ball was that he couldn't *see* it. Matt had gamely been going out for the local Little League just like all the other sixth graders, but his performance at bat was wildly erratic. His later description of what it was like to be Matt at bat was pure black humor. He never had any idea when the ball left the pitcher's hand because he couldn't see that far. He would see a white blur approaching, looking more like a flying saucer than a baseball, and he would aim for the middle of it. Sometimes he connected and sometimes he didn't. There was a special tension in the air every time Matt was up. "That's looking them over, Matt!" the spectators would roar when he declined to swing at an absolutely perfect pitch. He simply hadn't seen it at all. "Attago, Scoop!"

When eye tests revealed that his vision was 20/200, glasses were prescribed and Matt's eyesight improved spectacularly. Carl and I were terribly upset that this condition had not been discovered earlier, and felt like bad parents. Wherever his desk was in the classroom, he was always getting up to go to read the blackboard, but no teacher ever seemed to think there was anything strange about that. They always thought he was extra intelligent because he always got the answers right. Thus for years he had disguised the blurriness of his vision with his intelligence. It was typical of him that he never complained, assuming that the world looked fuzzy to everyone.

Shortly after the Willis boys arrived, it became obvious that the kitchen would have to be enlarged. In the process, our attention was turned to the small attic above the kitchen, which was reached by murderously steep, almost vertical stairs and served as a passageway to the bedrooms beyond. It occurred to us that a dormer added to the little attic would provide more usable space, and we would have five bedrooms instead of four upstairs for the teeming multitudes.

Matt asked for the new room, having already agreed to relinquish to John his high-ceilinged room with the bookshelves and cabinets that Carl had built in. The shelves were now full of John's athletic equipment, and it didn't feel like home to Matt anymore. So Matt got the little room over the kitchen at the top of the steep stairs. He figured out how to make the farthest reaches of it habitable, the part that was behind the chimney under the sloping eaves and therefore not in the traffic pattern. Everyone but Nelly and Paul had to bend over to get back there, but Matt didn't mind, he said.

Matt's move to the attic behind the chimney over the kitchen, like so much of what happened those days, was full of double meanings and ambivalent motivation. On the one hand, he had achieved something that very few people in that house had then, a room of his own, and newly painted at that. But on the other hand, an inescapable fact remained: it was the attic over the kitchen. A Cinderella story in reverse, with the sexes changed.

The cinders aspect of Matt's predicament did not manifest itself for all to see until many years later — 1971 to be exact, when, while living in a commune, he had a psychotic breakdown. He wrote a book about this experience that was published in 1975 and is now regarded as something of a classic in its field as well as a resource for families confronted with similar problems. It has given them hope because he got well.

Reading the book when it was first written, and then re-reading it in 1986 in the process of writing this book, I had to ask myself what the breakdown had to do with me. There were certain eerie resemblances between my short disorientation in the summer of 1958 (I wouldn't go so far as to call it a psychotic breakdown) and his longer one in 1971. Matt was always generous to his parents when discussing his breakdown, saying repeatedly, no blame, no blame, you didn't do anything wrong. Of course we *had* done things wrong; all parents do. But still, something wrong enough to cause this acute craziness at age twenty-two? It had to have been chemical. Still, his chemistry was our chemistry, wasn't it? Whether we were responsible for it or not?

As I pondered the similarities between my craziness and my son's, I came to understand us both on a deeper level. Both of our reactions had been coping mechanisms, in a way. Both were connected to realities that were challenging — threatening — each of our lives. Both were connected to a sense of power that was not altogether illusory.

I understood with a jolt that my "episode" had not really been over when it seemed to have been. I had emerged from it somehow different. Then, when the tragedy struck, I had dealt with it as well as I had partly because of a sense that my old self was somehow muted. It was as if I were in a daze for the better part of a year. I could do what I had to do, but it was not my old self doing it. That explained why it was necessary to become someone else even to begin writing about it. I had managed to submerge my own needs and most of my old feelings in service to my new family and my new obligations. Of course I had periods of negativity when it had all seemed just too much, of sorrow and rage over the necessary losses I had undergone. But I had not acknowledged them at the time; I had put them down. If I had acknowledged them, I would not have been able to do the job. I was all sweetness and light and optimism and positive thinking in the face of the disaster, simply because I had to be.

I ended up thanking God for *expedient insanity.*

Then I saw that maybe Matt's had been an expedient insanity as well. It had removed him from a situation, both physically and psychologically, that he had to get out of in order to grow. And he had grown, and I had grown.

Both episodes had an essential alignment with objective reality and with some higher power. I knew this to be true. My mistake, in the living of the experience, had been in trying to interpret it too literally: Russian refugees in the attic, indeed! A baby in the barn! But both of these figments of my imagination were partially true. I had only gotten the details wrong.

What Matt got wrong I'm not quite sure about. He was younger and with no real responsibilities other than to himself. His sickness was more acute, less chronic, less tempered by experience.

Matt rose from the cinders like the phoenix.

By the end of the summer of 1971, he was permanently out of the hospital and at work on his book, which took another three years to finish. In 1973 and 1974 he took pre-med courses and then was accepted at medical school. He graduated in 1978. Meanwhile, he had met Hannah in 1973 and married her in 1975. Gregory was born in 1977 and Jacob in 1980.

Matt practices medicine now, and is as responsible a family man as a man can be.

16

Amy

But even with comfort and courage beside her, Nora couldn't think of a way. "Must I do it myself?" she asked.

The earth began to rumble.

And truth bloomed from a daisy.

"Yes, Nora, you must do it yourself. You can do anything."

> **From Amy's story called "Nora's Tale"**

Amy, nearly nine when she acquired her four new brothers, was on the brink of the realization that there was a momentous and fascinating difference between the sexes. It was *true* that boys were different from girls! Furthermore, she was beginning to think that, all things considered, she liked them better. It seemed they came in more distinct and astonishing varieties, whereas girls seemed to her all more or less the same.

Just as she was reaching this stage in her development, she got all these new brothers – a whole laboratory of boyhood to aid her research on the subject. Amy was a natural at it. She was cute, lively, talented, smart, friendly, and still innocent. It was clear that she was about to be beautiful. At the moment of her birth she had come into great riches of body, mind, and spirit, so riches came easily to her. It seemed utterly natural that she should get so many extra brothers, since brothers were nice things to have. Not being in any particular need, she would have gotten along very well without them, but still, they were awfully nice to have. That was the spirit in which she welcomed them into her heart and her home, and it made for wonderful relationships every which way. At the time. The difficulties came later when it turned out that none (well, very few) of the men in the big world quite came up to the flavorful variety of her own brothers. But that is another and a later story. At the time, Amy was in heaven. There was no one to compete with, since no one shared her special temperament or capabilities. She was apparently not displaced in any way by the event, still being the oldest, prettiest daughter.

With each of the boys, Amy developed a

unique relationship. Ned, being so much older, was like a father confessor. She divulged things to him she would never have told her own father – or her mother, for that matter. In return, she received what seemed to her at the time a much more mature form of protection than she had ever known before and vast funds of hitherto unimagined information. Ned just plain knew more than her real big brother. He was a treasure trove of both useful and arcane data. So he became super big brother, putting Matt, who had been as good a big brother as a twelve-year-old could be, in the shade. Ned, in turn, was delighted to have this promising little cousin/sister under his tutelage. The more young minds he could bend to his exotic ways, the better.

As for John, he provided an entrée into sporting circles she had known nothing of before. Suddenly, all the football, baseball, and basketball players not only spoke to her, some even became infatuated with her. And John was so handsome. All her friends fell in love with him, and that was fun because it enabled her to become a source of information for them. Amy soon became the queen of a clique of the best-looking, most popular girls in town, lining up for a look at a hero. This group later became known as the Herd. Where Amy was, the Herd was. And where the Herd was, the best parties were, and the most fun. It was unabashedly cliquish, something wonderful to be in and terrible to be out of. Amy grew to be ashamed of this later, but at the time it was utterly normal and the most desirable way to be.

And then there was Cubby, her peer, her never-failing companion. When the social intricacies of life in the Herd got too heady or too complex or too fatiguing, there was always good old Cubby for plain down-home friendship. Shier, younger girls who couldn't aspire to John fell in love with Cubby, and so she had that group clamoring for her attention and intervention as well.

And then, in case she was feeling more motherly than studious, flirtatious, or companionable, there was little Paul to take care of. Amy had her hands full, and it suited her completely. Luckily, she had an energy level equal to her multi-leveled new existence.

One might wonder how all this affected her relationship with the siblings she already had, and in that regard, too, the effects were nothing but good.

Before the cousins came, Amy had a bit of a mean streak. And, as in all families, it chiefly found expression in her dealings with her brother and sister. Amy was a strong-willed middle child with an inherently restless nature. It seemed to me that she was born squirming to be up and off and at it, whatever it might be. Whereas both Matt and Nelly as babies were more passively accepting of whatever attention came their way, Amy was always arching her back and wanting to be off doing something else. It wasn't that she was unaffectionate or inattentive; she just had a shorter attention span for whatever happened at that age. She needed a lot of challenge and stimulation to keep her interested. Her middle-child syndrome, therefore, took a familiar route and then branched off into some interesting variations. The typical part was that she was always either too little or too big: too little to have the privileges that Matt had, too big to be babied like Nelly, always in the middle. But Amy was never one for being neither here nor there. For a time she compensated for her middleness by victimizing both Matt and Nelly, each in a different way. If things got boring, she could always create a stir by screaming that Matt had hit her or taken her crayons away or something equally uncharacteristic of him. She looked so adorable and was so convincing that she often got away with it, and Matt would be unjustly punished. Her alternative remedy for the tedium of daily life was the enslavement of Nelly.

Nelly adored her older sister and would un-complainingly do anything she asked, just to be adored back (which she was, mostly). Thus Amy figured out how to get back at Matt for being older and at Nelly for being younger, and all in all managed to stay entertained.

All of this had its unattractive side, which Amy was the first to admit when the first glim-merings of reasonableness set in. Fortunately, this stage did not go on very long, or it might have developed into a habit. It was the advent of the Willises, along with a rudimentary sense of justice, that broke the pattern. Sud-denly there was *so much more* to think about than just torturing her brother and sister! Amy plunged into her new cousin/sister role with her customary dedication. There was no more time for being mean to Matt and Nelly. She was through with that for life.

There were even more bonuses for the orig-inal siblings. Suddenly they .ere a team, too. The new team had just moved in, so the old team got it together to make them feel welcome. Matt and Amy, for the first time, really, could pool their resources to make the newcomers feel at home, and Nelly could tag along, saying, "Me, too, me, too," like a mascot, although she had no understanding whatever of what was going on. If it was all right with Matt and Amy, it was all right with her.

So the born-again teammates looked at one another with new eyes. We're in this together, brother and sisters, so let's do the best we can. And they did.

Matt's sense of protectiveness toward his little sister was not extinguished by the coming of the cousins. Instead, it was rewarded by her acceptance, finally. He might not be her *only* protector in this new world, but he was her staunchest. In later years, when Amy genuinely needed rescuing, it was always Matt who did it. In the midst of what looked like the worst disaster the family had ever faced, brother and sister made friends.

The single most striking thing about Amy was that she could always draw circles around everyone in sight. Literally. When she was about two, she made some rather unexceptional marks on a piece of paper which looked something like an angel. At that point, her parents' marriage was on a relatively even keel. Carl's short stories were selling regularly, and we had an advance on his first book. Carl had made the move away from corporate public relations to a commitment to writing. We were beginning to feel settled down in the first little house we had bought on Cape Cod. In short, we had the time, as we would never have again, to pay close attention to what each of the children was doing. We thought the marks Amy made on paper were extraordinary, so we gave her more paper and more pencils and more crayons and more paints, and hung up everything she drew. This, of course, takes place in millions of homes when children, all of whom are creative to begin with, start to scribble. With Amy, the timing was particularly propitious and the encouragement she got inspired her prodigiously. The trauma of displacement by a younger sibling had not happened yet, so she hadn't had to learn any dirty tricks. All she had to do was draw. That was the beginning of angels, angels, angels everywhere.

One Christmas Eve years later, when Amy was twenty-five, she had a special Christmas Event for everyone to see. For heightened dramatic effect, people were allowed to see it only one by one, and they were not permitted to tell those who hadn't seen it what it was. She led us off separately into the cold night, down the road to the underpass over which Cape Cod's only railroad tracks crossed old Route 6A. There in the dark, wonderful glowing mystical angels flew this way and that, dangerously close to the pavement, but with the clear capacity for flying up and away. She and Nelly had crept out the snowy night before,

Nelly holding the paint bucket and flashlight and ladder while Amy drew the angels. It was a hurried job, as they had to hide in the bushes when cars came by. One neighbor threatened to call the police and have them arrested for defacing public property, but by then it was too late, and the angels were immortalized in black paint on white concrete. They have since been hopelessly besmeared and besmirched by teenagers with spray paint cans. Amy repainted them three times and then gave up.

As the angels matured and developed, along with Amy's own development as a woman and an artist, they came to have double meanings. Amy's angels had marvelous wings of all shapes and sizes growing out of shoulder blades as naturally as though that was what she actually saw when she looked at people. They also had tough, sinewy, sometimes chunky, sometimes sensuous bodies, very earthy bodies, painted in rich earth tones, often with stubby, undifferentiated feet clinging firmly to the earth or mired completely in it. One sat astride a huge, ungainly, friendly beast with sleepy eyes who didn't seem to realize he had an angel on his back. Others were carrying enormous loads. Furry creatures with long tails, curled up paws, and bemused expressions clung to an angel's back.

As the years passed, Amy's paintings of

women/angels carrying large loads proliferated and eventually became one of her trademarks. One show that opened in New York in 1981 had five such "load" paintings side by side: *Mother Load, Sister Load, More Than One Load, Charcoal Load,* and *The Last Load.* The angels in these paintings had lost their wings, as there was no room to paint them, what with the profusion of creatures creeping and climbing on and clinging to the angels' shoulders. In each of these, the woman/girl/angel has an expression somewhere between surprise and resignation, with a great deal of tenderness and just a touch of yearning — as if she wished she could find a good place to put down the load — but no bitterness. These angels are wondering how in the world they got on this particular planet in the first place. The obviously male creatures look utterly content to be where they are, adoring, docile, immobile, totally dependent, and very, very heavy.

With every "load" picture, the symbolism became more clear. All the evidence to the contrary, the very concept of maleness, made manifest in these paintings, must have been a burden to Amy from a very young age. You would not have known that by looking at her life, only by looking at her paintings.

Amy was a totally unconscious feminist

painter. When I went into my overtly feminist phase, mandatory in the seventies for someone whose forties marriage dissolved during that era, Amy was the one who argued with me the most. She hated the stridency of the movement and its clichés (which I did, too, but never mind, we argued anyway). Every time the feminist argument was put in words, Amy would react negatively; even so, with her hands she would be creating yet another picture in oils of what I was trying to say. The most striking example was her *Female Crucifixion,* a gorgeous, nearly life-size woman on a golden cross.

Amy's "load" pictures turned upside down the traditional view of women as dependents. In her paintings men were the dependents and women the more highly evolved beings tirelessly holding them aloft. What the women did was what mattered; what the men did was soak it up. It was the women who had the energy and the creativity, the strength, the patience, and the beauty. A lot of people who admired the paintings for their style and grace and what they liked to think of as whimsicality seemed entirely to miss the message.

The message was about more than the contrast between men and women, of course. It was about the duality of creatureliness and the angelic, body and soul, how inextricably mingled they are in human beings, and what a puzzle it is. The loads became interchangeable, the angels patiently lugging their creatureliness around with them, the creatures, in turn, from time to time holding up the angels. Or tempting them. A later phase had creatures and angels tempting each other. Angels could be seen in dirty places, like the New York subway, stark naked amid the graffiti, with a fish or a bird or a swan in their laps, completely above it all and totally ignored by fellow passengers. Eventually, some of the angels turned out to be men, tempting earthly girls to look in their direction. Some would and some wouldn't, and some were simply scared out of their wits. Who ever knew what was going to happen next? Certainly not Amy, but she drew them anyway. Beginning very early, so early that it was impossible to say when, Amy recorded in her painting her own ongoing battle between worldliness and transcendence, the story of her life. The story, in some measure, of all our lives.

At an even later stage, the angels began to lose their wings in excruciatingly overt ways. One angel with a broken wing, on crutches, looks longingly out over a salt marsh, trying to figure out what made her fall down and break her wing. Another, even sadder angel, sitting naked and forlorn on a New York street corner, has amputated her wings and laid them out on a gold and turquoise checked tablecloth on the sidewalk. They are for sale along with the trinkets, broken crockery, old shoes, and used paperbacks, the flotsam and jetsam of other ruined lives. We are all angels, Amy is saying. But that is not to say it's easy. Some angels make it and some don't.

When my marriage with Carl began to break up in 1970 — Began? I say to myself. You know very well that it began to break up before it started. How about 1945? Oh, well — when that part of the breaking up that occurred in 1970 began, Amy was the first of the children I told. I was in such a state of pain, confusion, and disorientation that it was not a very clear telling. But Amy, who was twenty-one, understood instantly. She had known since she was nine. We sat in the dark, empty living room with the candle drippings from past celebrations soaked into the rug, and we wept. The tears seemed to make the old, hardened candle drippings glisten again.

"But it's not just you, Mom," Amy said. "It's all of us. We've all been dumped. He left us all."

It was too big a load.

In 1974, Amy and Nelly took a trip together

across the country. At the time, Amy, disillusioned with her own poor first marriage and with life when she looked at it soberly, was drinking too much and experimenting with drugs. Nelly was disillusioned for other reasons, mainly feeling abandoned, and had almost stopped eating. We feared she was anorectic. When they stopped for a lunch break, Amy would buy a six-pack of beer, Nelly an apple.

In Colorado they took peyote together. Strikingly similar frightening images came to them simultaneously. Amy saw herself as a furry little creature, all flesh and blood and energy, scampering mindlessly about on a river bank, like a beaver or a woodchuck. She saw the beautiful surface of the river, gurgling and sparkling in the sun, and she thought, "Oh, good. I'm going in there to splash and play and play." Then, when she got in, all sunny and happy, she suddenly realized that there were dangerous things under the surface of that pleasant river. Demons were under there!

"Oh! I'm in danger!" she thought. And she scrambled out as fast as her furry little legs could carry her. She got away just in time, from what she wasn't sure. Then she looked up and saw Nelly on a ledge above her. Nelly didn't look right. She was blue and white, too blue, too white. Against the sky, she was almost transparent. Her hair was dry and silvery and blowing weightlessly. She looked as though she were about to leave the earth. There was so little flesh on her bones, so little blood in her veins, she was about to float away forever.

The real Amy reached for the real Nelly's hand. So carefree a moment before, now her heart was pounding and tears were streaming down her face. "Oh, Nelly," she said. "I'm afraid you're going to die."

Nelly looked at her sister, her eyes so blue in her white face, and said, "I know. I see it, too. And look at you, so full of blood, so full of *life!*"

The sisters held hands and wept, each terrified for the other and for herself. The vision was so clear.

"Don't go, Nelly. Not yet. Please don't go yet." Amy, heartbroken, pled for her sister.

Nelly, without saying a word, had pulled Amy out of the dangerous, deceptive river. By sheer will power Amy now pulled Nelly back down to earth.

They each had been about to die in completely different ways. Each saved the other. And it has been an ongoing salvation. Though it took some more time, Amy left alcohol, drugs, her faithless husband, and her bad marriage behind. She got out of the fearsome river.

Nelly, also taking her time about it, put on

some weight, got the red blood flowing in her veins again, and planted her feet on the solid earth. She decided it was too soon to float away.

17

Nelly

Where do I belong
Other than
In this state of dazzle?
From Nelly's journal

Back to 1958 on the time loom that this story
has become: there was in the original family
one remaining set of priorities and expectations
to be upended. Baby Nelly, almost four, was
unceremoniously the baby no longer. It was on
this age level that the only open antipathy was
manifested. Nelly accurately perceived that her
only real enemy among the bewildering array
of new "brothers" was Paul, who was attracting
undue amounts of attention from everyone.
Her room, which her father had transformed
into a magic blue and pink and white bower by
building a wooden canopy with hearts and
flowers and stars to surround her newly acquired grown-up bed, was turned back into a

nursery with a crib and a changing table and a potty seat and all the other accouterments of infancy to receive Paul. Regression! Betrayal! Nelly's bed was moved into Amy's room, where it immediately lost its dignity. Nelly had to move her toys and her clothes as well onto Amy's terrain, where there was no space for them and where she was not only resented but enslaved on account of it.

Poor Nelly. No one had time to consider in depth the feelings of a four-year-old who was unpracticed at speaking up for herself. As with all household proceedings at that time, the move was prompted by simple necessity: there was nowhere else to put Paul. Nelly didn't know what to do except to hit him every chance she got, which was frequently. Paul, in turn, promptly recognized his one true adversary, and he could bite and he could scratch. He learned to use his fingernails, as other small animals do.

They were both amazed. Neither one of them had ever experienced overt hostility, either in him or herself or in anyone else. So neither of them could believe the terrible reality into which they had been plunged. They would sit cross-legged on the floor, methodically inflicting grievous injury on each other, screaming with rage and pain at each swift and certain retaliation. Left alone for any length of time, they would surely have done each other serious physical harm. Nelly was bigger and stronger, but Paul's teeth and fingernails were sharper, so it was pretty much a draw. Rough parity prevailed, as in the Soviet-American arms race.

Fortunately, someone always intervened, dragging the frazzled and humiliated little creatures off in opposite directions to nurse their wounds and plan their counterattacks.

I surveyed the situation from each Lilliputian point of view, and ended in despair of their ever being able to tolerate, let alone love, each other. Two world views had been toppled. I had not yet fully absorbed the old adage about time healing all wounds. Twenty years later, Nelly and Paul did become friends. But it might not have happened had they not been separated for most of the intervening nineteen.

When Paul went away to the Deep South in the spring of 1959, Nelly wondered for five minutes what all the fuss was and then went about her business, which was to allow her own inherently amiable nature to develop. She got her room back. She put her dolls and stuffed animals and books and clothes back where they belonged and snuggled in, closing the door between her room and Amy's. But her security had been darkly threatened and remained deeply shaken. The effects of the trauma, as with those of the other children, would take years to play themselves out. Nelly thenceforth had to deal unconsciously with what has come to be referred to in psychological parlance as "survivor's guilt." She had won the contest. Paul had disappeared. Had she killed him?

Nonetheless, Nelly proceeded to grow into a wise flower. She looked like the angels that Amy was always drawing. Her hair was a honey-colored mist, like a halo askew. Her eyes were a clear azure, translucent as a perfect June day. If she had a negative feeling or a worrisome thought, you could see it cross her face, dip into her eyes and out again, like a stray cloud. She never tried to hide what she was feeling and thinking, having early given that up as impossible. This is not to say her feelings were not deep; they were simply immediately apparent, like rainbow trout at the bottom of an ice-clear New Zealand pool. Nelly was a gorgeous transparency. Which was hard to maintain under such burly circumstances.

A fragment from my favorite Shakespeare sonnet would sometimes play on the fringes of my memory as I watched my youngest daughter grow:

How with this rage can beauty hold a
plea,

Whose action is no stronger than a
   flower?
O how can summer's honey breath
   hold out
Against the wreckful siege of batter-
   ing days
When rocks impregnable are not so
   stout
Nor gates of steel so strong but Time
   decays?

How indeed?

When Nelly invaded her room, Amy decided
that her eyelashes were too long. This was true,
if you were Amy, among whose many attributes
luxuriant eyelashes were not included. Nelly's
azure eyes were framed with a sweep of maple-
sugar-colored lashes so long and thick that one
had to wonder how she kept her eyes open. So
Amy got a pair of scissors and asked Nelly to
hold still so her eyelashes could be appropriately shortened. This was perfectly all right
with Nelly, who only wanted to be Amy's
friend. If Amy wanted to cut her eyelashes, it
must be eyelash-cutting time.

But Amy's basic sense of morality came to
the rescue. She relented at the last minute and
told Nelly she was only fooling. We found out
later about the near loss of Nelly's eyelashes

and chalked it up as more of the same: sibling rivalry on the rampage, providentially dispelled before someone really got hurt.

Nelly was the classic beauty of the two, while Amy was "the cute one." Naturally, each spent countless formative hours wishing she were the other. The wonder is that Nelly grew up convinced that she was ugly, stupid, ungainly, untalented, and just generally a person whom no one wanted to have around. Beautiful, intelligent, gifted, loving, and alert, she never guessed that these attributes might apply to her. Amy, of course, had similar self-negating thoughts, but she didn't let them show until much, much later.

Several years after the worst of the crisis, I came across this terse, undated message floating in the debris of Nelly's outgrown things:

> Dear Nellie
> I am sorry that you have been a bad girl so I have to give you some coal or noththing I am very sorry
> From Santa Claus

The note was in the same handwriting as Amy's 1959 diary.

On top of having to fight for her life with both Paul and Amy, Nelly came to the conclusion that her parents didn't like her all that much either. The third child rarely gets as much attention as the first two. In Nelly's case, this quite ordinary condition of benign neglect — measurable by the relatively few photographs of Nelly as a baby, compared with the many of Matt and Amy — was enormously accentuated by the advent of the four orphans. Our combined attention span, already fragmented by time, parenthood, career, and each other, was shattered into so many shards and splinters by the demands of our expanded family that poor little Nelly bloodied herself trying to pick up the pieces.

But she was not as fragile as she looked. She held her own. She picked no favorites. She beheld all her older siblings with the clear-eyed gaze of one who was there to learn. Suffering the indignities, inequalities, and mortifications of all youngest children, which were magnified in her case, she learned from them. She started consciously trying to "grow up" when she was four, which, of course, was too young. "C'mon, Nello. When are you going to grow up?" was the frequently uttered complaint of the older sophisticates around the place. The injustice of it! No one had asked *them* to grow up at four. Naturally, she cried a lot. Getting Nelly to cry was so easy it early on stopped being a favorite household sport; there was no challenge in it. She could never tell whether she was being teased or they were serious, so her eyes instantly filled with tears, and then they were sorry.

Nelly had such an oversufficiency of high-powered role models that it was impossible to sort it all out. She tried on all styles before she found her own. No matter what she did, she was always the baby relative to everyone else, a state that was periodically profoundly depressing to her. She would go bopping along like the others, serenely independent in her friendships, her art work, her school work, maintaining a creditable rear-guard action in all areas — and then she would wilt, like a flower without water.

So she would go elsewhere for nourishment for a while. Nelly had several best friends who belonged to more traditional families with generally lower age and energy levels, where the competition was not as keen, at least for her. These families, as if acting out of some ancient tribal wisdom, simply took her in from time to time, providing her with other-mothers, other-fathers, and an extended peer group of other-brotherly and -sisterly beings.

Not the least unexpectedly, Nelly became the world traveler of the group. She would suddenly decide it was time to go somewhere, and off she'd go: to California, to Mexico, to Jamaica, to Guatemala, to Italy, to Crete, to Israel. She would work for a time as a waitress or a weaver or a vacuum cleaner salesperson or she'd sell a piece of her art work. And then she'd take off with a backpack, some vitamins, a list of addresses, that flowerlike innocence, and an infinite capacity for acquiring brothers and sisters. By the time she was twenty-one, she had been to more places than everyone else combined, and had friends of all races and classes everywhere. John, at the same age and looking ten times more worldly, had barely made it to New Hampshire.

She would come home from her exotic destinations with marvelous adventures to tell, but she could not get anyone to ask her where she'd been. When she'd returned from an archaeological expedition to central Mexico, where she stayed with the Tarahumara tribe as part of a team that discovered the most impressive relics of the Olmec civilization — later exhibited at the National Gallery in Washington and the Metropolitan Museum in New York — her siblings barely registered the fact that the baby had been away for a while.

The desert was her favorite place. Nelly became a desert flower. A wise desert flower. She had the tender toughness that it took to be one. She was full of tough love, in the best sense of that phrase.

So it was no accident, was it, that eventually, in Jerusalem, Nelly found Jesus Christ.

She had always been the seeker of the group, spiritually as well as physically, asking questions, demanding answers, never letting go until she had received at least a minimally satisfactory response. As each new cultural adaptation hit her generation – Transcendental Meditation, est, yoga, macrobiotic dieting, pumping iron, all kinds of heavy-duty exercise – Nelly would try it out, get something out of it until she discovered its inevitable limitations, and go on to the next thing. She would enter into each new discipline with high enthusiasm and an intensity unequaled by her siblings, who might try this or that but who did not have such high expectations of finding something that would make all the difference.

When Nelly found out about Jesus, she knew she had found the thing that made all the difference. She didn't pass on by, looking for something even better. She stuck with Him. She studied and learned. She associated with like-minded people. She found a church. She learned to pray with power. This was not just a steppingstone to the truth, but Truth itself.

I was there when her conversion experience happened. It was in February of 1979. Nelly had called me in Washington, late in January, from Jerusalem (where I had no idea she was; I thought she was picking grapes in Crete) and said, "You've got to come here, Mom. It's the heart of the world."

I didn't know what she meant, but I knew she was on to something, and that she was right. I had to go there. Part of me was surprised, surprised yet again. Another part of me had always known that a suggestion like this could only come from Nelly.

We had an incredible month together, traveling the length and breadth of that tiny country. She had learned how to get around both the Old City and the new one like a native. She introduced me to her new friends from all over the world, most of them émigrés, some of them born in Israel. We lived for a week in a newly restored house in the old Jewish section of the Old City, just a few winding blocks from the Wailing Wall. We rented a small car and traveled east and north, all around the Galilee, staying in nunneries and monasteries for a few dollars a night, with never a reservation anywhere, subsisting on felafel and olives, delicious and nourishing.

We rested a few days in Jerusalem and then

rented another car and went south, along the Red Sea and into the Sinai. We made a friend on the road, and with his guidance and help climbed Mount Sinai. Yossi taught us how to make bread over an open fire at the seashore, how to make soup in an old battered pot in the moonlight, from a few potatoes, onions, and tomatoes scrounged from a friendly Bedouin. I have never had more delicious soup. We found the rock that Moses smote. We found the place where the burning bush was and walked barefoot around and around it, trying to imagine how it could have looked on fire, with the sun coming from here, no, from there! No, earlier, no, later! We never did figure it out, but in that place it was not hard to imagine. We slept in a base camp at the foot of Mount Sinai that we never would have known about, much less gotten into, without Yossi speaking for us in Hebrew. Adventure piled on adventure. Everything was touched with magic. And the ancient red rocks of those old mountains looked down on us like patient patriarchs, blessing us in our levity and our seriousness, as if to say: It's all right with us. This place is for you, too. This place is for everybody.

With all of that as a background, and with only two days left of my visit, the high point was yet to come. Again, it was through the mediation of a stranger. We were on a bus in Jerusalem and asked the driver to let us off at the most convenient point for walking to our hotel, the American Colony, a luxury we had allowed ourselves for our last few days. A stranger sitting behind us leaned forward and said he would be glad to walk us the few blocks to the hotel. "It is not a safe neighborhood, you know," he said. We knew, but we felt safe anyway. I must have looked surprised and said what anyone would have said: "How kind of you. But you needn't. We'll be fine. We know the way." But he persisted. "I want to be sure you'll be all right. Isn't that the way we're meant to be? Isn't that what Jesus said?"

At that point, I must have looked astonished. Nelly turned around to see who was offering to go out of his way to protect us. We were looking at a thoroughly Jewish face. Talking about Jesus on a bus in the Arab section of Jerusalem?

"Surprised, aren't you?" he said. "I happen to be a Christian."

"So are we," I stammered.

"I guessed," he said.

So Mr. Z walked us to the hotel, which was twice as far as we thought it was, and on the way he told us his life story: how he had lost his wife and his child, how he had found his faith, how dangerous it was to be a Jewish

Christian in either the Jewish or the Arab sections of Jerusalem, how he loved the Psalms and the hymns. He sang one while he was at it, quite loudly. No one attacked. He ended by inviting us to a Bible study meeting at his church the following evening.

We were both intrigued and confounded. It would be my last evening in Jerusalem, and we already had plans to visit another one of Nelly's newfound friends, to say goodbye. Nelly looked noncommital.

I found myself saying that of course we'd love to, but we had other plans, that it would take some figuring out, that we would either meet him in the lobby of the hotel at seven the next evening or leave word for him. He bowed in a most gentlemanly way and left, humming "Amazing Grace."

When I asked Nelly whether she wanted to go to the meeting, she said she really didn't think so, that it was too complicated. But wasn't he an amazing person?

So I left a note at the desk the next morning before we left for our daily travels, thanking him but telling him we wouldn't be able to join him.

That evening, our visit with Nelly's friend ended sooner than we thought it would, and we found ourselves on another bus headed for the American Colony Hotel. Nelly suddenly said, "I think I'd like to go to that church meeting after all."

I said, "Well, we have time, but we don't know where it is. And it's too late to go find Mr. Z."

Nelly said she remembered that it was the Baptist church in that neighborhood. We were nearby, and a person sitting behind us said, "It's the next stop. A block to your left."

This time we didn't even see who had spoken. We got off at the next stop.

We were greeted at the church, a small white building set back from the street, by friendly people who wanted to know what had brought us there. We told them about Mr. Z (who wasn't there yet, but showed up later), and they nodded understandingly.

The church slowly filled up, and then it began. There were hymns sung in Hebrew, and the sound was glorious. Then there were personal testimonies, and people discussed parts of Scripture that had particular meaning for them just then. A Swedish woman had an especially moving story to tell. The congregation was asked if anyone there had anything to add. Then it happened. Nelly's hand went up. I looked at her sitting next to me, disbelief on my face. This is my shy Nelly, my desert flower, with something to say to these strangers in a distant land.

"Something just happened to my heart," she said. "I just want you to know that something amazing is happening in my heart." She was holding both hands over her heart, as if to keep it within her. "It has been all hard and crusted over," she said, "but now I can feel it cracking open. Listening to you just now, my heart has a crack in it." Tears were streaming down her face. I wanted to hold her hand, but her hands were too busy keeping her heart in her rib cage. "I don't understand this at all. I think I need help. My mother understands all this" — she looked at me with a kind of sob — "but she's leaving tomorrow morning. She's been trying to tell me, but I haven't understood. I still don't understand. All I know is this strange thing that is happening in my heart."

Nelly was immediately surrounded by those sweet people, laying their hands on her, stroking her blond hair, comforting her and rejoicing, telling her they would help.

It was utterly astonishing. Here was another of my prayers answered, hard and sharp and sudden, "a gauntlet with a gift in 't." Another miracle.

I left Jerusalem the next morning, knowing that Nelly would get the help she needed, then and in the days to come. Her path has not been easy. It never is. The continuing frustration of her life is that, as she tries to tell her siblings about this adventure, they keep on not hearing her.

But as her interest broadened and her commitment deepened, sure enough, the clouds in her life began to dissipate. She was able to leap over hurdles she had thought insurmountable, as if her feet had wings.

Do I speak too easily of miracles? Forgive me. The thing about miracles is, they accumulate, like little drops of water making a mighty ocean, like little grains of sand making a beautiful land. To perceive one miracle clearly somehow opens up one's vision for others. You begin to know how to recognize them. Sometimes they are modest little things. Then you say thank you. Then more occur.

It's as if God and nature *like* having their more subtle effects noticed. So they play to every newly awakened sensibility, and before you know it, miracles are everywhere. Like angels.

18

The Baby in the Barn

Some good, sacred memory, preserved from childhood, is perhaps the best education.
Feodor Dostoyevsky
The Brothers Karamazov

Twenty-eight years have gone by since the events took place that have prompted this reminiscence so filled with pain and joy. As I approach the end of it, I ask myself what I have learned from those years, now that so many things have come full circle.

My own children are now the age that I was when the four boys came to live with us. Amy is exactly thirty-six, as was I in 1958. She has a baby. The baby lives in the barn.

The house is filling up with children again — six grandchildren, seven by December, when Nelly has her second child. The oldest grandchild, Gregory, is now the same age, nine, that

260

Cubby was when he came to our house. This is hard to believe. It is all so hard to believe.

Just as of old, the six children, five boys and one girl, swirl and sweep in and out of the house and yard, up and down the steep back stairs, appropriating their parents' old rooms to play in and sleep in, their old clothes to dress up in, their old toys to resurrect and make into something new. They make exactly the same noises. The two-year-old says no, loudly and constantly; the three-year-old might as well be a truck, when he's not an airplane; the five-year-old has found his father's old harmonica and from it comes, nonstop, the theme from "Batman." The seven-year-old, the only girl, has reached the age of relative calm and reason. She pats my arm a lot and says, "I hope you're feeling better." And the nine-year-old, the father of them all, makes nearly adult noises, like "Cool it, Jacob" and "Be quiet, Eric."

Who are these new people, these links to the future? Matt married Hannah, and they begat Gregory and Jacob. Amy married Joseph, and they begat Andy. Nelly married Luke, and they begat Eric. Ned married Billie, and they begat Alana. Cubby married Natalie, and they begat Jack. John has neither married nor begat anyone yet; but he will, he will, in his own good time. Meanwhile, he is everyone's favorite uncle. He's the one with a Jeep. Paul married Libby; as yet they have no descendants.

Each of these seven little families is a book unto itself, of course. But not for here and not for now. Enough to say that the stories of the parents are not even half over; the stories of the children have only just begun. And that they all have each other. The curiously alive old house helps make that possible. They keep it alive, and it them. The sacred memories collect.

Amy and Joe have remodeled the barn so that it is a year-round home. It is beautiful; there is no more junk in there. Andy's room is in the loft, where hay used to be stored. I always knew there would be a baby out there someday. But how could I have known that he would look like Amy and have Joe's eyebrows? I only had the details wrong.

There is another sense in which things have come full circle. This story began with the double deaths of Annie and Ned. I have reason to think that it won't be long before it will be time for me to make that journey, catch that train. Maybe not. It's a question of knowing and not knowing at the same time. Life is ever surprising, so I also won't be surprised if I am given more time. But facts are facts. And the fact is that I have the same sickness that Annie had. I've had it for the four years it took to write this. It comes and goes. It is the same sickness I dreamed about in 1958. What I didn't know then was that it would get me, too. I didn't need to know then. Now I do.

So what is there to say when you know you don't have much time left? Or rather, what is most important to say, since you can't say it all? I wrote this partly to find out what I might have to say. And in the doing I have discovered how absolutely madly in love I am with life and with all the people I was given — yes, given — to love. I am grateful to have learned so much of life: of the steadiness of personalities, the constancy of love, the preciousness of the moment, the fragility of time, the power of the imagination, the strength of that vital life force that enables us to hold each other up when our wings get broken. And perhaps, above all, I've learned that pain and joy are inextricably mingled, and that out of suffering does come love. It is a great mystery to me why this should be so.

But I know that there will be angels in the next underpass as well, and I am content.